FAIRHOPE YACHT CLUB
75 Years of Memories

A PICTORIAL HISTORY

BARBARA HAYES BROWN
AND SARAH JOHNSTON COX

THE
DONNING COMPANY
PUBLISHERS

Copyright © 2017 by Fairhope Yacht Club
101 Volanta Avenue
Fairhope, AL 36532

All rights reserved, including the right to reproduce this work in any form whatsoever without permission in writing from the publisher, except for brief passages in connection with a review. For information, please contact Fairhope Yacht Club.

The Donning Company Publishers
731 S. Brunswick
Brookfield, MO 64628

Lex Cavanah, General Manager
Nathan Stufflebean, Donning Production Supervisor
Richard A. Horwege, Senior Editor
Chad Harper Casey, Graphic Designer
Kathy Snowden Railey, Project Research Coordinator
Katie Gardner, Marketing and Production Coordinator

Brad Martin, Project Director

Library of Congress Cataloging-in-Publication Data

Names: Brown, Barbara Hayes, author. | Cox, Sarah Johnston, author.
Title: Fairhope Yacht Club, 75 years of memories : a pictorial history / by
    Barbara Hayes Brown and Sarah Johnston Cox.
Description: Brookfield, MO : The Donning Company Publishers, [2017]
Identifiers: LCCN 2017001089 | ISBN 9781681840918 (hard cover : alk. paper)
Subjects: LCSH: Fairhope Yacht Club (Fairhope, Ala.)—Pictorial works. |
    Yacht clubs—Alabama—Fairhope—Pictorial works.
Classification: LCC GV823.F35 B76 2017 | DDC 797.124/606—dc23
LC record available at https://lccn.loc.gov/2017001089

Printed in the United States of America at Walsworth

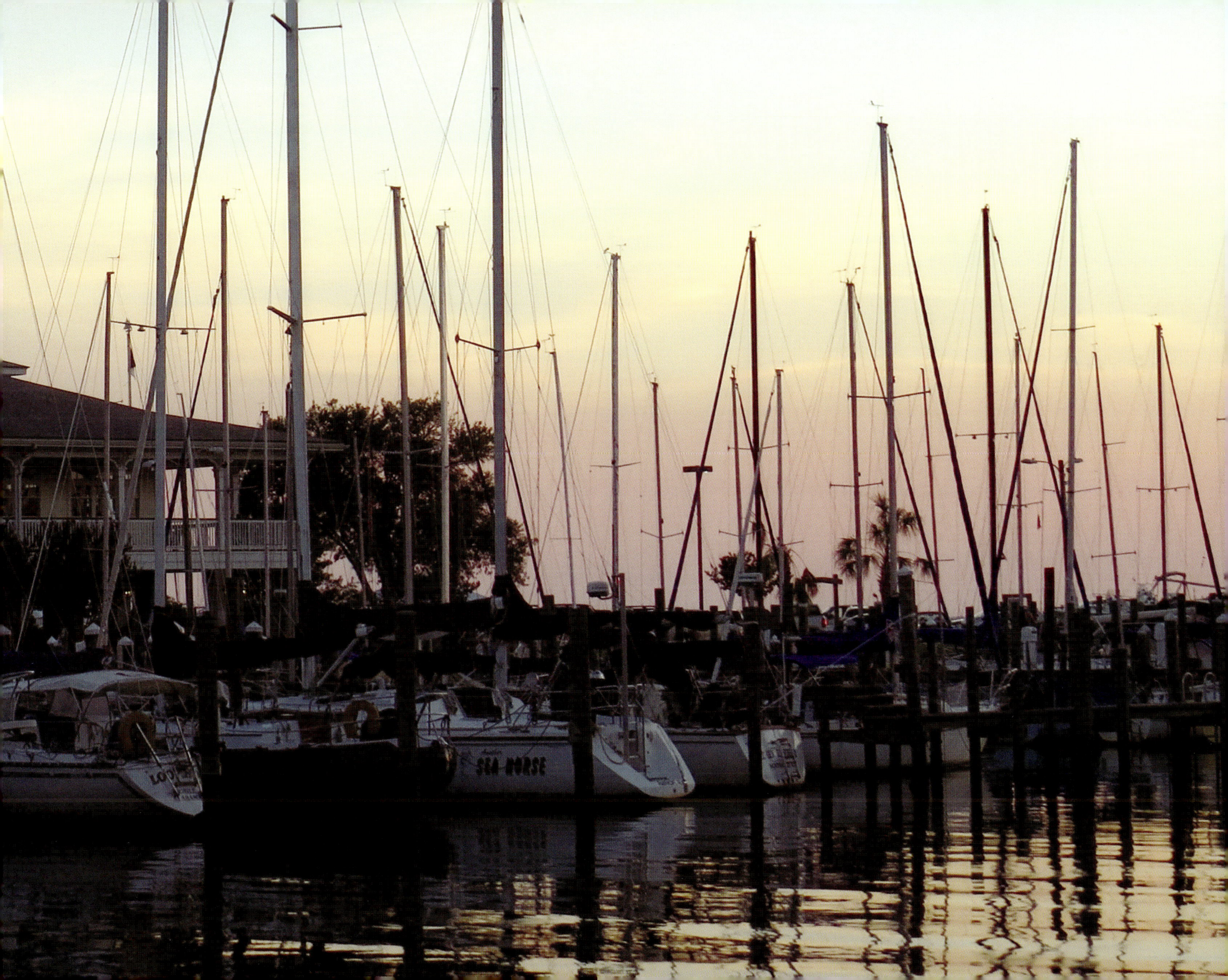
SEA HORSE

Dedication

This book of photographic memories of Fairhope Yacht Club from the past seventy-five years is dedicated to the founding members and to all the volunteers who have worked tirelessly to preserve the legacy left by them. It is intended to honor the memory of these members and their families and all those who came later and continued the work.

With a commitment to the vision held by the early members for the future of Fairhope Yacht Club, these volunteers donated their wisdom, their time, their money, and their skills. Through their shared love of yachting in all its forms, they have kept Fairhope Yacht Club on course and sailing into the future on a fair breeze.

Contents

Acknowledgments... 8

Introduction... 9

Chapter 1: Bayou Volanta... 11

Chapter 2: Anchors Aweigh... 17

Chapter 3: Harbor... 27

Chapter 4: Storms and Flooding... 37

Chapter 5: Early Boats and Boating... 43

Chapter 6: Gulf Yachting Association... 51

Chapter 7: Races and Regattas... 61

Chapter 8: Fairhope Yacht Club Junior Sailors... 83

Chapter 9: Families and Social Activities... 95

Chapter 10: Commodores... 109

Chapter 11: Hurricane Katrina and Beyond... 117

Chapter 12: Sailing into the Future... 137

About the Authors... 144

ACKNOWLEDGMENTS

We are indebted to the previous historians for their gift of an extensive collection of photographs documenting the early days of Fairhope Yacht Club. In putting together this book, we were able to utilize many of the old photographs which they had preserved. We also wish to express gratitude to the members who took these photographs and to the people whose activities were recorded for us.

We relied heavily on this treasure trove which we supplemented with a few additional photographs from Fairhope Yacht Club members' family collections. Our thanks to the Baroco, Bung, Johnston, Koppersmith, Marty, Nestor, Reynolds, Yeager, and Zadnichek families for sharing their precious family photographs with us and to Donny Barrett of the Fairhope City Museum.

Richard Prolsdorfer, who had worked as a Publicity Archivist at Century Fox Studios in Los Angeles, at the American Film Institute, and at ABC Television, provided us much needed technical support and assistance in the creation of the precursor of this book, the film, *A History of Fairhope Yacht Club*. These same skills and talents have been valuable assets to us in the development of *Fairhope Yacht Club, 75 Years of Memories: A Pictorial History*. We appreciate the knowledge and experience he shared with us in these projects.

INTRODUCTION

This volume, *Fairhope Yacht Club, 75 Years of Memories: A Pictorial History*, is a collection of photographs taken over the past seventy-five years presenting the story of families coming together through common interests and a shared vision. The waters of Bayou Volanta and Mobile Bay served as a center of activities for these friends and were an integral part of their lives. It was their hope to create a special place there on Bayou Volanta as a lasting gift to future generations.

We have selected the photographs that we thought the reader would like to see, that best represent the work and play of these individuals and their families, that best tell the story. We have used few words in this volume. The words are used only as a support for the pictures. While the photographs capture only fragments of the whole story of how Fairhope Yacht Club came to into being, we believe they offer glimpses of the bits and pieces of a time and place now gone.

Our intent is to create a pictorial journey which answers questions about the origins of Fairhope Yacht Club and its early members and which provides readers with a source of information about how the club has grown and changed over the past seventy-five years. Traveling through these pages the reader has the opportunity to get to know these people and to appreciate their contributions to the Fairhope Yacht Club of today.

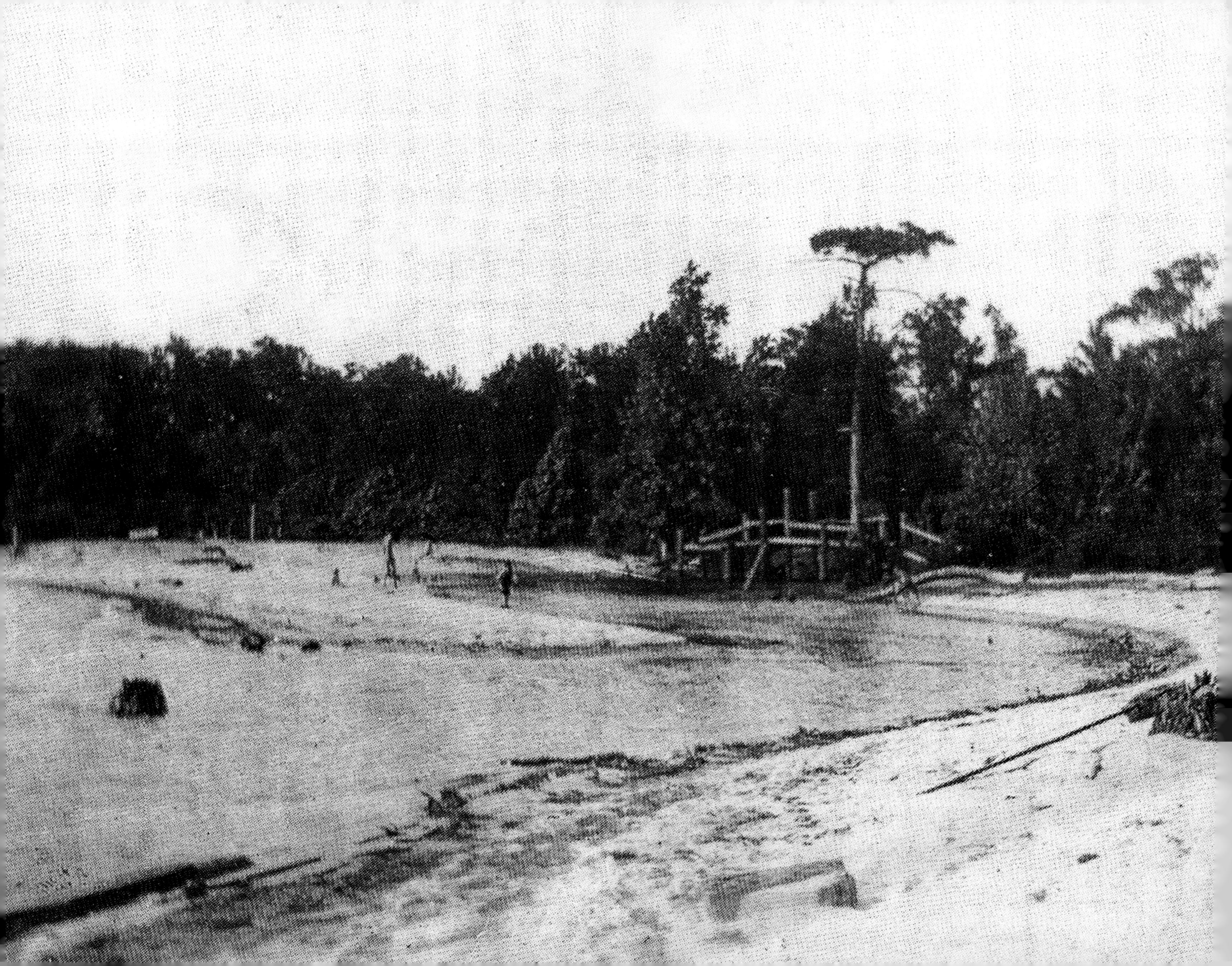

CHAPTER 1
BAYOU VOLANTA

Drawn by the swift flowing streams of sweet water surrounded by high bluffs on the eastern side of Mobile Bay, Native Americans had seasonal campsites and permanent villages. They were followed by a succession of Europeans who visited and explored the area along the shore. Where Bayou Volanta (Flying Creek as it originally was known) met the bay, early travelers came to fill water casks for their ships. Later settlers came to build camps for soldiers to rest and recuperate from various wars, and to establish large plantations. Eventually in the nineteenth and twentieth centuries, the land was subdivided and building lots were sold to families, businesses and hotels.

Going from a rapid flow upstream through the clay bluffs to a slow meander along the beach front, Fly Creek made its way into Mobile Bay. A popular destination for local inhabitants and visitors, its waters provided a respite for many on long hot summer days and an escape for anyone seeking repose on its banks. The small Sea Cliff Post Office can be seen in the background in this photo.

Top left: Families gathered to enjoy the cool waters on the sand bars at the mouth of the creek on the edge of Mobile Bay. Remnants of the old bay boat piers can be seen in the background in this photograph.

Top right: People took pleasure in simple activities such as strolling along the beach at the mouth of the creek.

Bottom: Boating was another form of recreation for these families.

Top left: Footbridges that were built in deeper places along the creek provided access to both sides. This view looking out towards Mobile Bay shows that some boards were loose and could be pulled back onto the supports to allow boats to go back and forth from the creek to the bay.

Top right: In this serene setting a lone lady angler relaxed at her favorite fishing hole.

Left: These children were enjoying the makeshift diving boards attached to one of these bridges.

Throughout the early part of the twentieth century, Fly Creek would attract many to its banks to cool off and swim at one of several prime swimming hole locations. This family may have traveled to the creek in the car seen near the bridge.

Both piers and bay boats are now long gone. Old pilings from these piers remain standing in this early twentieth century photograph.

Before the completion in 1927 of a causeway across Mobile Bay to the Eastern Shore, large bay boats ferried passengers and cargo from Mobile to various locations in Baldwin County. In the Fly Creek area there were two of these long bay boat piers. One landing was on the north side at Sea Cliff and another was on the south side, near the location of the Volanta Hotel.

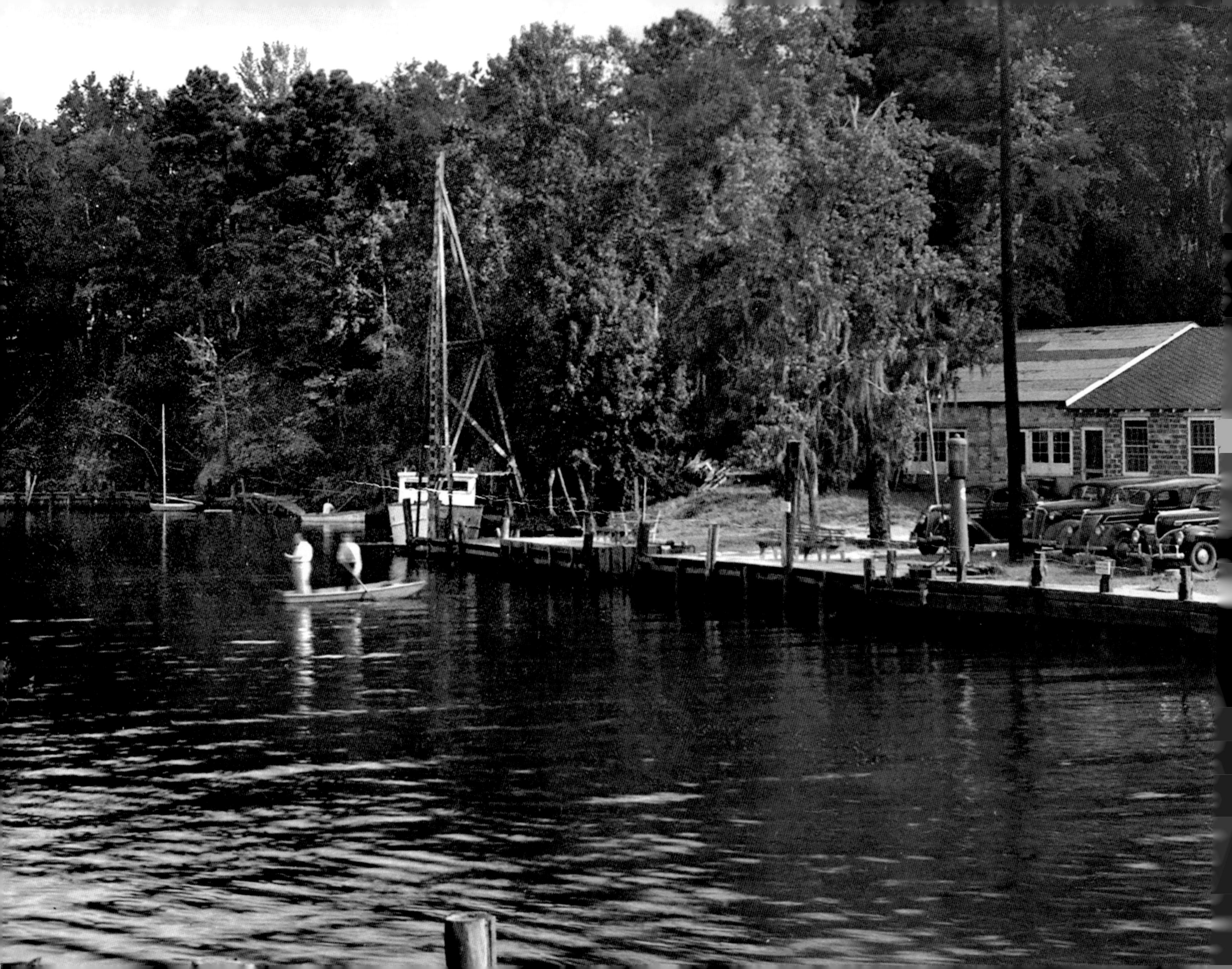

CHAPTER 2

ANCHORS AWEIGH

On the south side of Fly Creek, there was a popular swimming hole frequented by local families who swam, picnicked, and visited. In the 1930s three families who owned parcels of land there were the Wadewitzs, Godards, and Berglins. With a shared love of boating and fellowship on the water, they wanted to create a lasting legacy for their families and friends. Lead by Otto Wadewitz, who had been Commodore of the Racine Yacht Club prior to relocating to Fairhope, they came together to form the beginnings of a yacht club. Donating their Fly Creek property to be held in common, with Commodore Wadewitz at the helm, these three men, along with several others, created a corporation that became Fairhope Yacht Club in May of 1942.

Mission Statement

The Purpose of the Fairhope Yacht Club is to support and encourage the sport of yachting, including sailing, racing, power boating, and cruising; to provide good fellowship among its Members and to encourage good sportsmanship and boating safety.

Otto Wadewitz was elected the first Commodore. Some of the other men who formed the original corporation served on the first Bridge and Board of Governors.

After incorporation, Fairhope Yacht Club would grow rapidly. Then World War II intervened. Commodore Wadewitz's own motor yacht the REX was requisitioned by the Coast Guard, along with many other larger vessels on America's lakes and waterways and coastline, for the duration of the war.

37·B·301

After the war, the Secretary of the Navy, James Forestal sent Otto Wadewitz a letter thanking him for the use of the yacht, which had given valuable service in the war effort. In recognition of the service rendered, Commodore Wadewitz was authorized to display on the yacht two chevrons indicating the length of service with the Coast Guard.

The original clubhouse was a small clay tile building (formerly a fish house) situated on the property. In this early photo an upstairs apartment built onto the side of the bluff behind the main building can be seen.

As the membership grew, donated funds and volunteer labor would allow for additions to the original structure. In 1943, the first addition was completed and furnishings added. This view was taken from the north side of the creek and showed the early additions. Additional adjoining parcels of land also were acquired over the next decades.

Other Improvements to the original clubhouse were slow but steady. During the 1940s porches were added along the front of the building and on the side facing Fly Creek. Then tile flooring was installed to allow for dancing and so on. It was in the early 1950s that the clubhouse was enlarged again, followed by other modifications after that time. This view from the west side showed the "new" additions.

Member donations of materials and supplies and volunteer labor were vital to the continued success and survival of the early club. Sidewalks and landscaping were being added here to enhance the grounds.

The fruits of their labor are evident in this photo. There were large cruisers docked in the background and the porches now had jalousie windows to replace the original screening.

Top left: While many social activities took place in the modest building, for a long time more formal events would be held at other locations in Fairhope that were deemed more appropriate for the occasion.

Left: This group was gathered in the clubhouse around one of the many square tables in use then. They were seated under the old ship's wheel chandelier. Some of these tables remain in use today, as is the wheel which is mounted in the present dining room to memorialize deceased Past Commodores.

21

Dedicated employees always played a key role in building Fairhope Yacht Club.

Top left: Another group is shown having a small party at the club. The photos on the wall show some of the sailors and the trophies they won. These photos are used in this book.

Left: Interior improvements were ongoing, but there was no working kitchen in the little building until the early 1960s. Of course, there was a bar from the beginning.

22

In the mid-1970s, equity members were asked to purchase a $300 bond to finance a complete renovation of the interior and exterior of the Fairhope Yacht Club building. This photo shows the newly updated dining area with the repurposed old ship's wheel chandelier.

After Fairhope Yacht Club finally installed a working kitchen, members were able to order meals and dine in relative comfort. In 1965, a Saturday night menu offered Chicken and Dumplings—Adults $1.00, Children 50 cents.

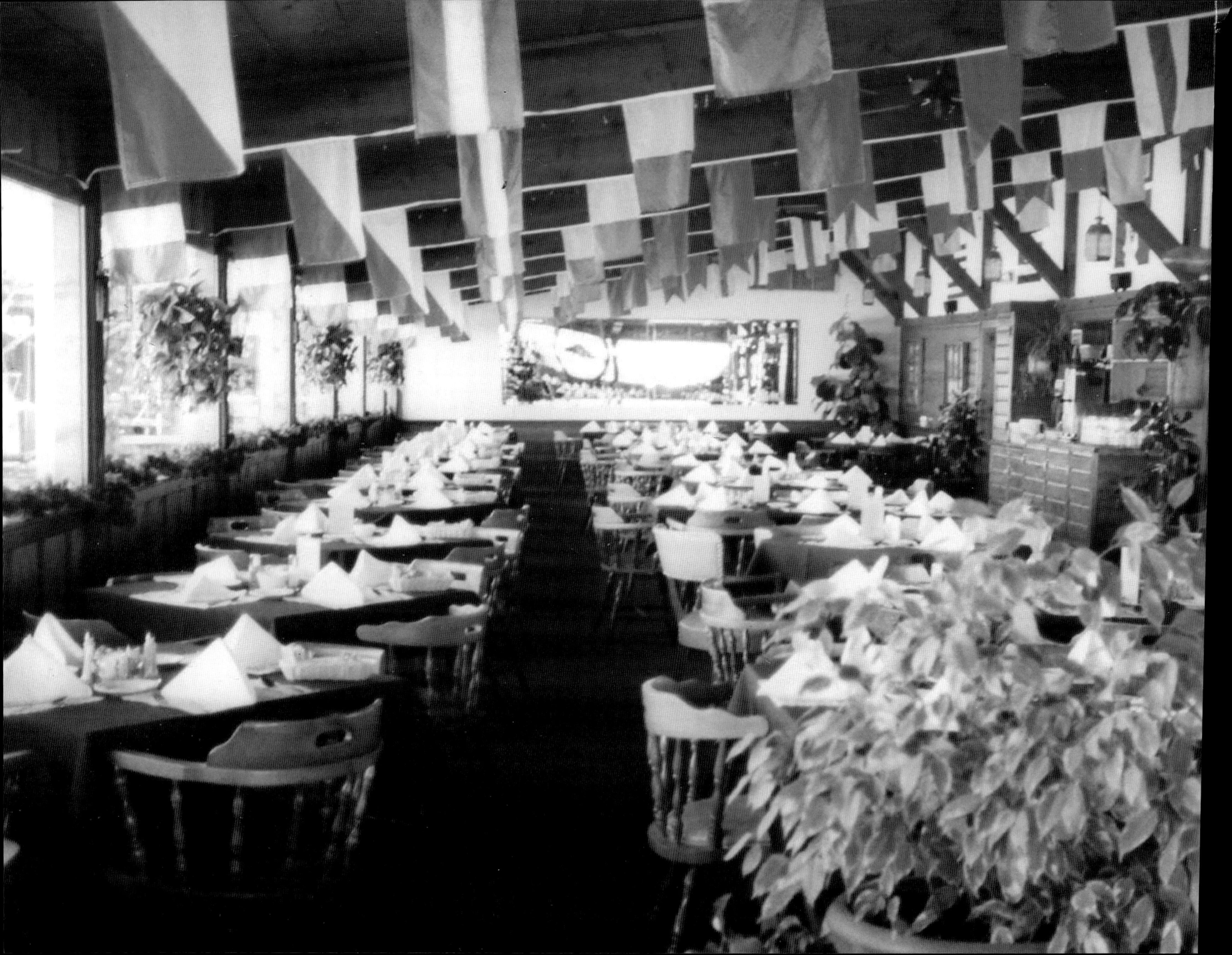

Here is another view of the dining area as it appeared in later years.

The slow but deliberate rate of development and improvement of the building and the grounds over more than sixty years would carry the members of Fairhope Yacht Club through countless storms, floods, repairs, and upgrades.

25

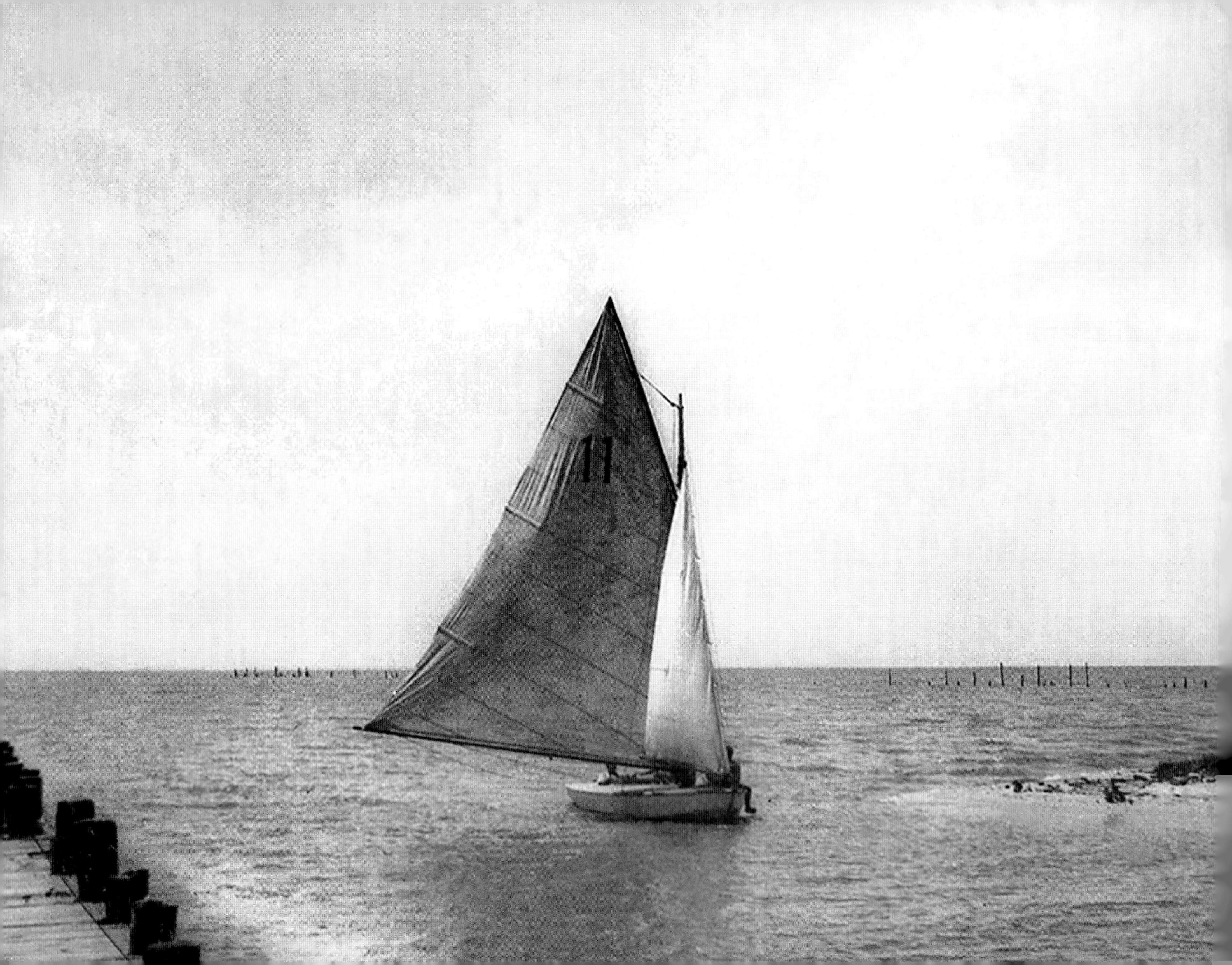
11

CHAPTER 3

HARBOR

Of the numerous streams entering Mobile Bay on the Eastern Shore, few if any provided a safe harbor or easily navigable waters. Shallow waters out many feet from shore presented problems for boats of any size or draft in their approach. Access for larger boats was limited.

In the beginning boats could enter the waters of Fly Creek only at high tide. There was no bulkhead, no dredged channel, no protected harbor.

There was an initial dredging funded by the members in 1943 to deepen and widen the mouth of the creek. This dredging created a fifty-foot-wide channel, seven feet deep extending approximately five hundred feet out into Mobile Bay and up into Fly Creek to the first bend. Pilings were purchased and set to mark the channel and to construct a breakwater. With member provided labor and materials the first bulkhead was built.

Below: Now larger boats could enter and exit Fly Creek.

One of the larger boats was the motor yacht owned by Otto Wadewitz. He brought it down the Mississippi River to Fairhope Yacht Club from Lake Michigan after World War II. The Rex was 49.5 feet long and turning it around in the newly dredged 50-foot-wide channel always was a bit of a challenge.

Not long after the initial dredging, storms and shoaling filled in the creek. The next dredging was provided by the Corps of Engineers in 1945. They dredged a channel into the mouth of Fly Creek that followed the original path of the creek, curving to the south side of what is now the Fairhope Yacht Club island and pool area.

In the early 1950s, a six-hundred-foot-long concrete bulkhead was installed. This new construction would be washed away shortly thereafter in a disastrous rain that caused extensive damage both to facilities and boats. The first breakwater that had been constructed earlier had already been washed out into the bay.

Above left: Boats of all sizes benefited from the increased access provided by the dredging. A dredge can be seen on the north side of Fly Creek. There were dredges in many of the photos over the years.

Above: A safe harbor also had been created on the north side of the creek for docking members' boats.

Numerous visiting boaters came to Fairhope Yacht Club after the dredging taking advantage of the newly created access and safe anchorage provided on Fly Creek.

A later dredging of Fly Creek in the early 1960s brought changes to the topography of the area and totally changed the configuration of the Fairhope Yacht Club harbor.

FAIRHOPE YACHT CLUB
FAIRHOPE on Mobile Bay ALABAMA
is honored to present

THE FINAL RACES
FOR THE
WOMEN'S NORTH AMERICAN SAILING CHAMPIONSHIP
NORTH AMERICAN YACHT RACING UNION
1965

This was the dredging of what became known as the "new creek." The dredging did not follow the original path of Fly Creek. Instead, it cut a straight path from Mobile Bay to the east, creating one large island where the pool and numerous boats slips now are located and two small islands. The dredging continued on up to the Fly Creek bridge.

This photo from the early 1960s shows the Fish Class boats docked at the pier leading to the large island that had been created by this dredging.

The two small islands created during this time can be seen in the background in this photo. One of these islands was known as "Pram Island" where the small boats were stored.

Top left: This photo was taken from the north side of Fly Creek where a Stauter Boat with hydrafoils cruised about in front of the small islands and the old clubhouse which can be seen in the background.

Left: In this photo you can see the Rhodes 19 fleet at Fairhope Yacht Club in the 1970s. The Juniors' Cabana can be seen in the background.

A later aerial photo shot of the Fairhope Yacht Club harbor showed that the two small islands had been supplanted by docks, boat slips, and finger piers. Only the large island remained.

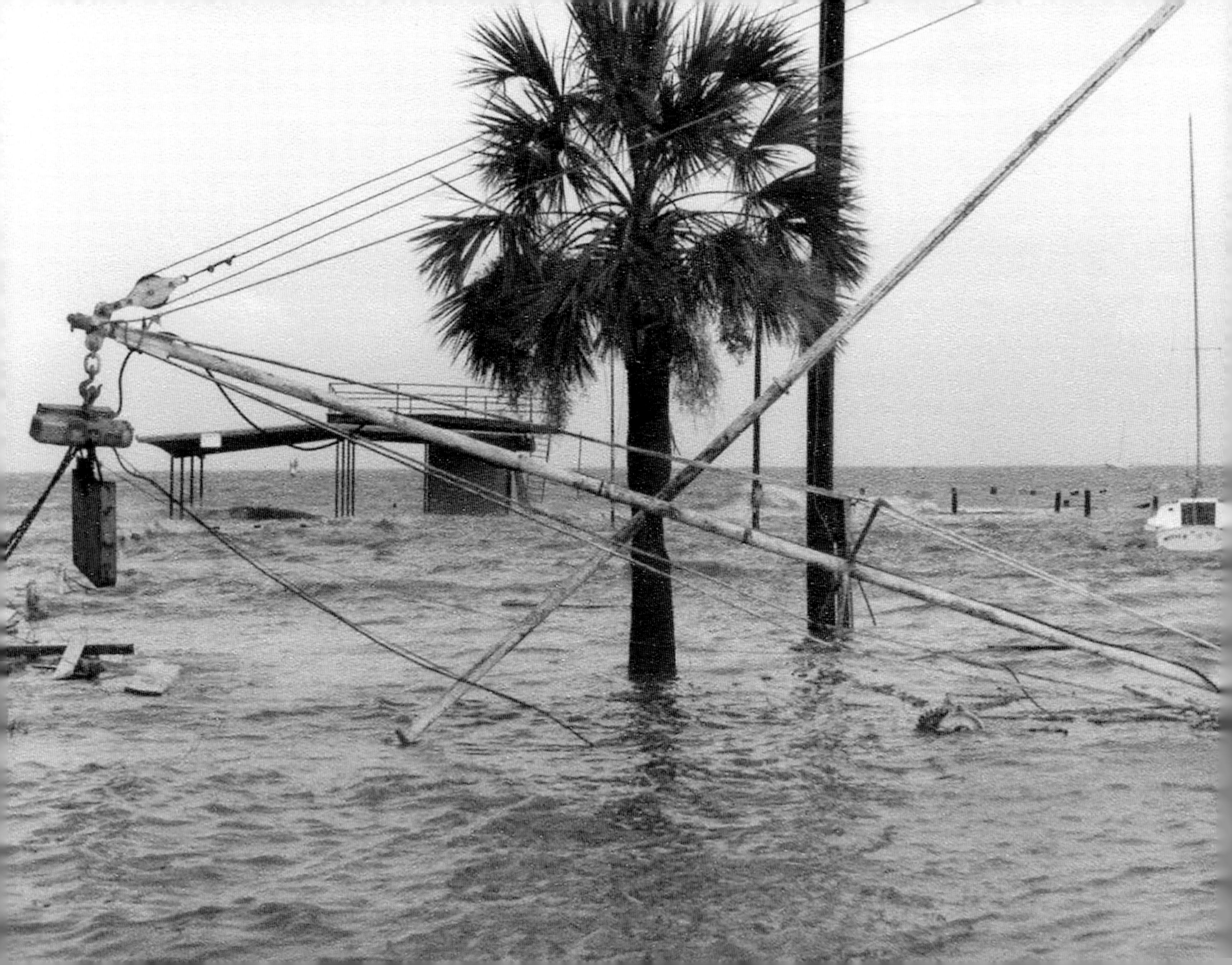

CHAPTER 4

STORMS AND FLOODING

Each decade brought dreaded storms to Fairhope Yacht Club; some unnamed, some named, some infamous, but all remembered for their respective destruction. Each storm would clog the creek with an onslaught of debris and necessitate clearing the waterways. This was in addition to the dredging required due to normal shoaling.

Effects from an early storm can be seen in this photo. Debris from both Mobile Bay and Fly Creek covered the property. Not long after the founding of Fairhope Yacht Club in the early 1940s, a flood wiped out the newly constructed original creosote piling bulkhead. A concrete bulkhead eventually replaced the first one.

Shortly after its initial paving, the Fairhope Yacht club parking lot would be washed away into Mobile Bay by flooding rains, along with members' boats from the harbor and many native trees on the grounds. Such a scenario would be replayed throughout the history of the club.

The repaving of the parking lot and renovation of the grounds had been completed in 1969 only to be seriously damaged with the arrival of Hurricane Camille that August. Repairs to the grounds and harbor caused by the flooding rains of July 1978 were completed in late August of 1979. Hurricane Frederic arrived in early September 1979.

Right: Flooding rains often brought massive destruction to the Fairhope Yacht Club harbor, to the building, and to the grounds. This photo captures some of the damage wrought by one such storm.

Bottom right: Fortunately, few serious floods would plague Fairhope Yacht Club in the 1980s and 1990s. However, wind driven water still would cover the grounds and penetrate the clubhouse on occasion.

No season of the year was storm free. The Christmas wreath on the building indicated damage to the grounds in a December storm.

With each flooding, mud and debris would be washed up against the doors and into the building. Afterwards the carpet would be pulled up, the concrete block walls and floors hosed out and the old clubhouse would be made presentable again. The old structure seemed to be indestructible and impervious to permanent storm damage.

Flood waters in this photo surrounded the building and filled the parking lot.

With catastrophic weather events over the years, there would be dues increases and additional assessments to fund repairs. The level of flooding of the grounds and building shown here was a fairly frequent occurrence.

This pattern of destruction, dredging, repairing, and rebuilding would be repeated and would continue into the present.

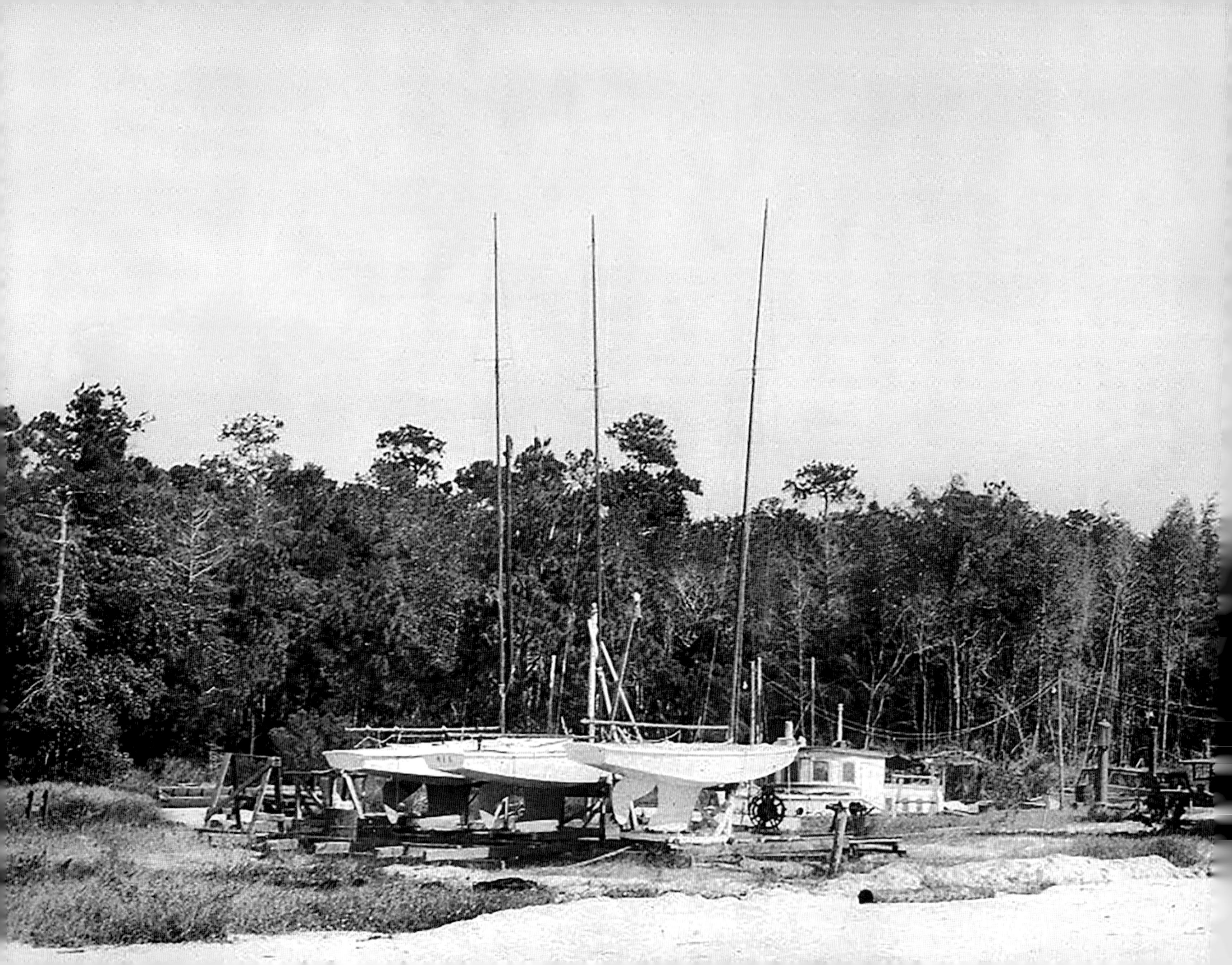

CHAPTER 5

EARLY BOATS AND BOATING

Boats and boating were an important aspect of work and play on the Eastern Shore of Mobile Bay. All kinds of boats and boating activities were an integral part of the development and growth of Fairhope Yacht Club.

Keel boats were stored on the boat ways. This consisted of metal tracks not unlike railroad tracks upon which the boats could sit and be launched and retrieved from the waters of Fly Creek using a hoist.

Most of the members had boats of one sort or another. One early method of dry storage is depicted in this photo.

43

The first Fairhope Yacht Club Commodore is shown with the fleet of Star Class boats on the boatways in this photo. The Star Class boats were privately owned.

Top left: Shortly before the formation of Fairhope Yacht Club World War II began and had a significant impact on every facet of daily life for all Americans. Wartime gas rationing meant there was limited motorized boating.

Top right: So most members made do with what they had for the duration.

Bottom left: Many members of Fairhope Yacht club were one design sailors. In addition to the Star Class boats, there were other one design classes of privately owned sailboats at this time.

Bottom right: One of these was the Penguin Class.

Another one design group was the Lightning Class.

Far left: Some of the one design skippers, both men and women, attained national recognition for their racing skills.

Top right: Five Snipe Class boats composed the first Fairhope Yacht Club owned one design fleet.

Bottom right: Fish Class boats were the second fleet that Fairhope Yacht Club purchased. These boats were the one design boats that the Gulf Yachting Association required member clubs to sail in their sanctioned interclub regattas.

The Snipe had been designed in the early 1930s to meet a need for a small sailboat suitable for trailering that could be built at home from plank and plywood. At 15 ½ feet long, it was a simple affordable two-person one design racing dinghy that had an instant appeal to families with young sailors.

Fairhope Yacht Club was assigned the sail numbers 10 through 15.

Power boating and cruising were considered important components of yachting. Fairhope Yacht Club cruisers traveled to many of the same locations that today's members frequent, including Dauphin Island (before there was a bridge), Bon Secour, and the Fowl River area.

Some of these cruisers in Fly Creek here were part of the Eastward Ho group that traveled from the New Orleans, Louisiana area to ports in Florida in the last 1940s and early 1950s.

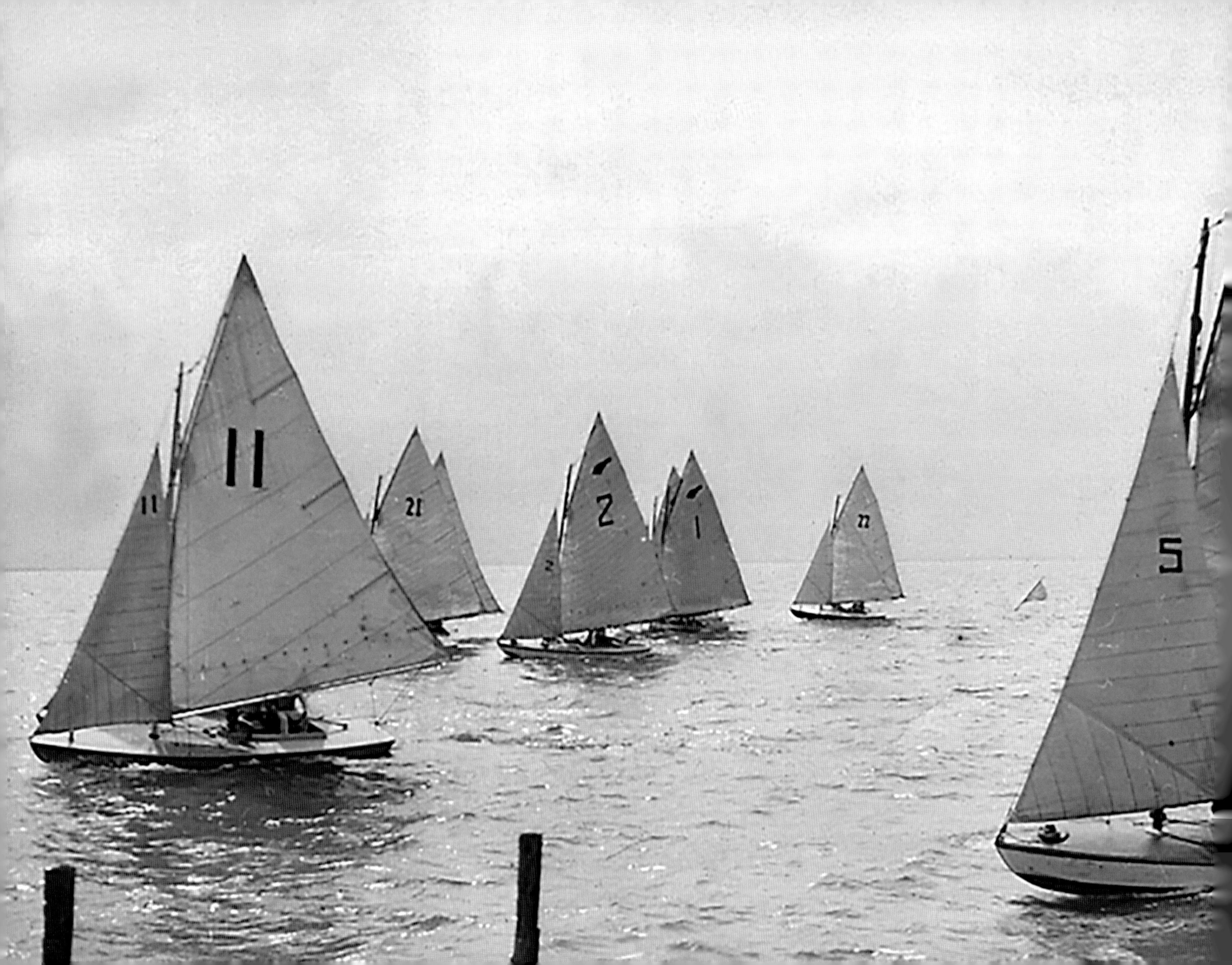
11
11
21
2
1
22
5

CHAPTER 6

GULF YACHTING ASSOCIATION

The forerunner of the Gulf Yachting Association had been founded in 1901 with member clubs from Mobile, Alabama, to New Orleans, Louisiana, but had ceased to function before World War I. The idea of consolidating neighboring yacht clubs into a union was brought up again and the various clubs reorganized as the Gulf Yachting Association at a meeting held in Mobile, Alabama, in 1920. There were five charter member clubs at this meeting: Southern Yacht Club of New Orleans, Louisiana; Pensacola Yacht Club of Pensacola, Florida; the Eastern Shore Yacht Club of Fairhope, Alabama, with members from Mobile and Fairhope, Alabama; Biloxi Yacht Club of Biloxi, Mississippi; and the Houston Launch Club of Houston, Texas. The Eastern Shore Yacht Club later transitioned back into the Mobile Yacht Club.

Fairhope Yacht Club joined the Gulf Yachting Association in 1944 as the eleventh member club. The clubs in the association ranged from St. Petersburg, Florida, to Houston, Texas. Fairhope Yacht Club members shown here were attending a GYA Meeting in St. Petersburg, Florida.

Being a member of the Gulf Yachting Association brought many benefits and opportunities for sharing common interests. One benefit was the reciprocity privilege which enabled members of each club to use the facilities of the other clubs in the association.

A copy of the 1944 GYA Lipton Challenge Cup Program listed member clubs competing in the races.

These Fairhope Yacht Club members were at St. Andrew's Bay Yacht Club in 1947, for one of the regular annual Gulf Yachting Association gatherings. There would have been meetings, parties, and one design racing scheduled.

Three major annual events in the GYA Calendar call for attendance by all member yacht club Commodores: The Opening Regatta which is held in early May, the Lipton Challenge Cup which is held in September, and the Winter Meeting which is held in January.

52

FAIR HOPE

Fairhope Yacht Club's one design Fish Class boats were flying wing and wing on a downwind leg in Mobile Bay.

Designed by the Southern Yacht Club Race Committee Chairman Rathbone De Buys after World War I to revive an interest in sailing and racing, the Fish Class boat was a small yacht that incorporated features of the New England Sharpie and the Biloxi Cat. Initially six boats were built and owned by Southern Yacht Club. The first race of Fish Class boats was held in June 1919. That same year Sir Thomas Lipton presented a trophy to the Southern Yacht Club which was to be dedicated to interclub racing in the Fish Class. The trophy became known as the Sir Thomas Lipton Challenge Trophy. In 1920 the first Interclub Fish Class Series was sailed and the announcement was made about the creation of the Gulf Yachting Association. The race which continues to be held each September has become the Lipton Series Challenge Cup.

The Fish Class boats were sailed in GYA interclub competitions for almost fifty years before another one design boat was selected.

A few years after joining the GYA, the Wadewitz Regatta, so named in honor of Fairhope Yacht Club's first Commodore Otto Wadewitz. The Wadewitz Regatta originally was scheduled yearly in the fall as part of the annual Fall Festival of Sailing at Fairhope Yacht Club. It continues to be sailed in the fall.

In this photo there are several Fish Class boats from different GYA clubs being readied for an early interclub regatta.

This photo captured other pre-race activities at the old gasoline pump along the bulkhead. Sails were being hoisted on the Fish Class boats tied there for a GYA Regatta.

A good wind blowing always made for a great sail on Mobile Bay.

Flying Scot Class boats were the next one design boat selected by the Gulf Yachting Association for interclub events. They continued to be used into the second decade of the twenty-first century.

In the mid-1950s, the Flying Scot was designed and built by Gordon K. "Sandy" Douglas as a nineteen-foot centerboard sloop used for both family day sailing and racing. In 1969, the Eleventh Annual Flying Scot North American Championship Regatta was hosted by Fairhope Yacht Club. This was the first year that the Flying Scot had become the official club boat for the members of the Gulf Yachting Association.

Top left: Flying Scot Class boats raced on Mobile Bay during major GYA annual events and in local regattas sponsored by one of the three yacht clubs there.

Bottom left: Gulf Yachting Association Commodores stood at attention at the flag raising ceremony for the Opening Regatta held at Fairhope Yacht Club in the 1980s.

Far right: In this photo burgees of the visiting GYA clubs were being flown at Fairhope Yacht Club.

Fairhope Yacht Club has had six members elected to serve as Commodore of the Gulf Yachting Association, including five Past Commodores. The other member who served as a GYA Commodore was the Commodore of the Eastern Shore Yacht Club who had called the inaugural meeting of the Gulf Yachting Association in 1920. He had served both as Commodore of the Eastern Shore Yacht Club and as Commodore of the Gulf Yachting Association prior to the founding of Fairhope Yacht Club.

Inset: In 2004, three women served as the first woman Commodore elected for each of the yacht clubs on Mobile Bay—Mobile Yacht Club, Lake Forest Yacht Club, and Fairhope Yacht Club. In this photo two of these Commodores were attending the 2004 GYA Lipton's Challenge Cup Regatta at Southern Yacht Club in New Orleans, Louisiana.

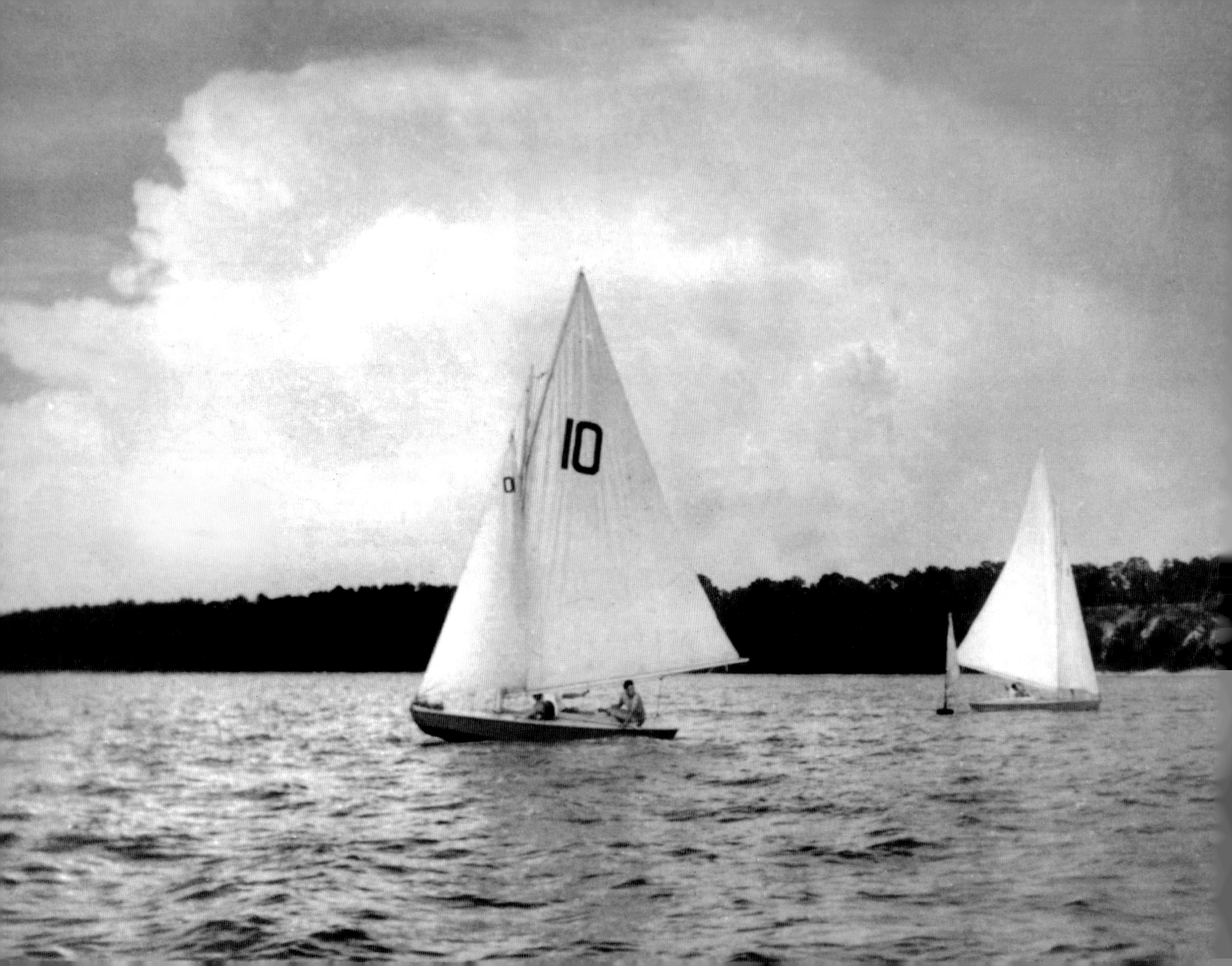
10

CHAPTER 7

RACES AND REGATTAS

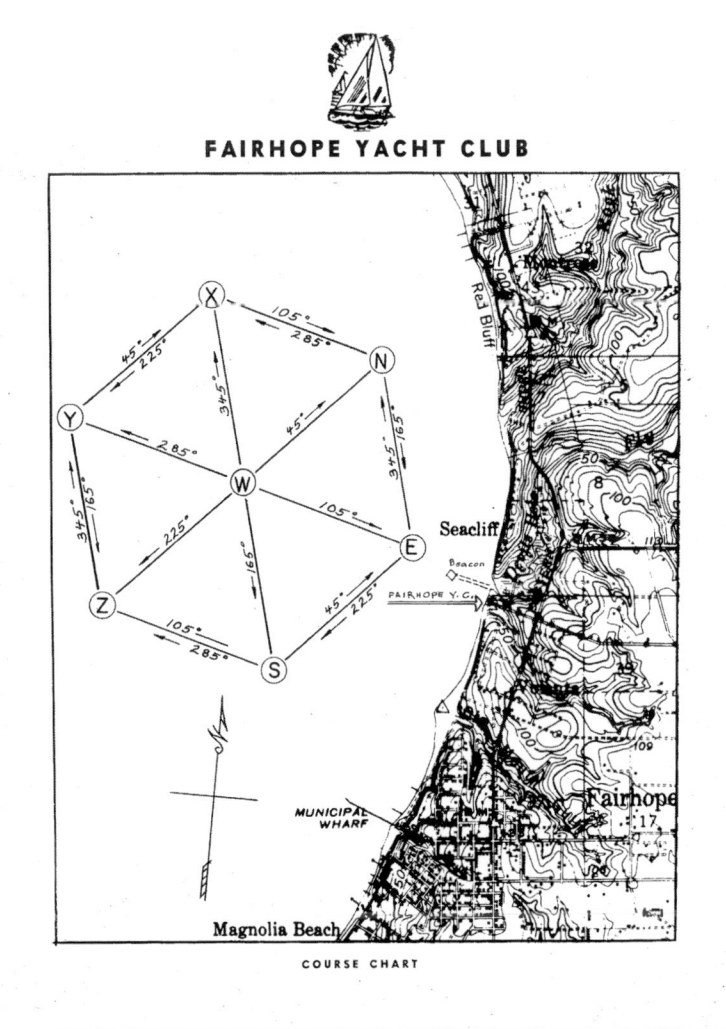

This is a copy of a course chart taken from a 1960s Fairhope Yacht Club regatta brochure. The designated names of the course marks have been changed over the years but the compass points continue to be rounding marks in local races.

61

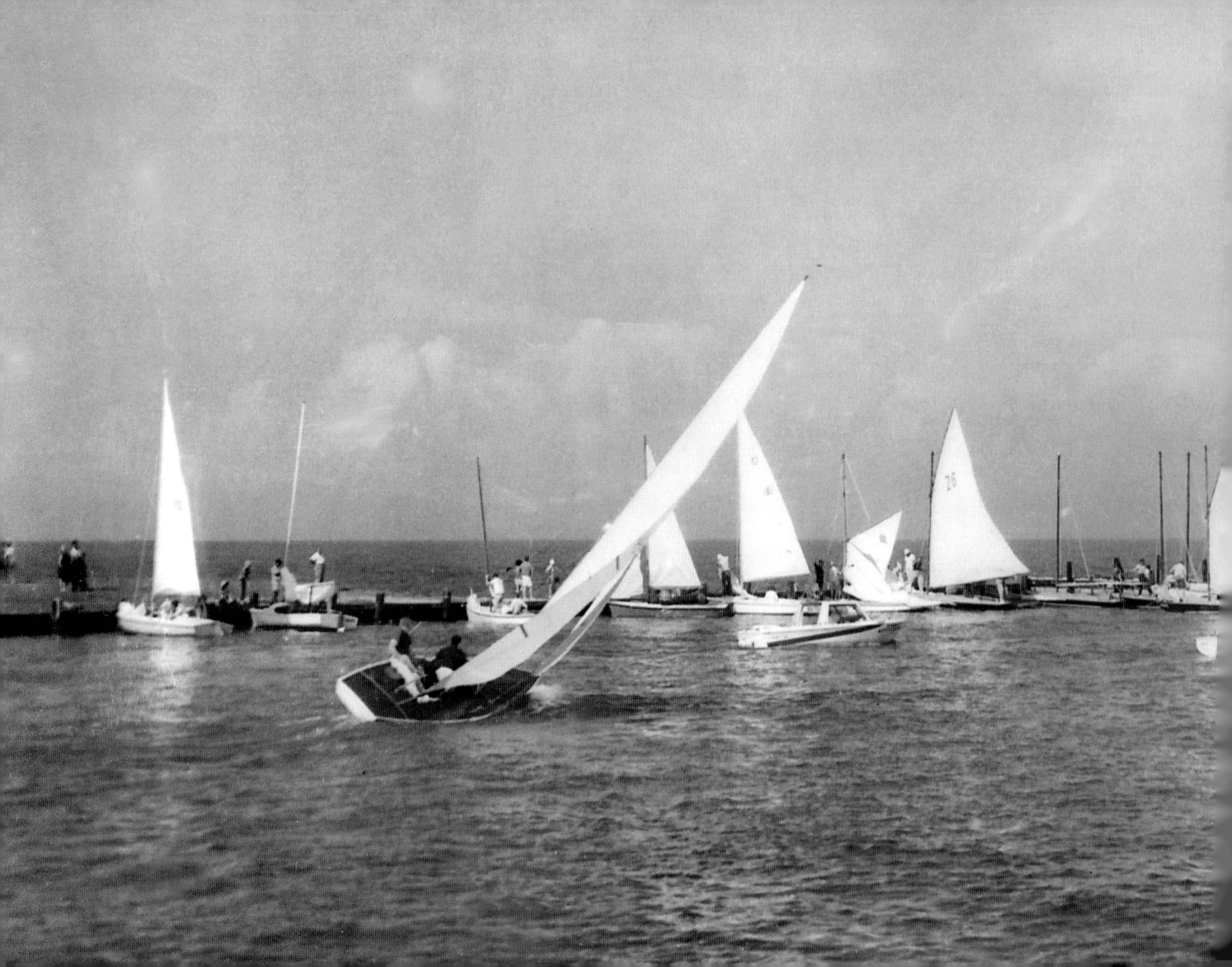
26

The 1943 dredging created dependable access for larger boats into Fly Creek. Soon after, Fairhope Yacht Club hosted its first regatta. In September 1943, thirteen boats participated, sailing a seventeen-mile course on Mobile Bay. This would start the tradition of a Fall Festival of Sailing for Fairhope Yacht Club. The GYA sanctioned Wadewitz Regatta originally was a part of this Fall Sailing Festival.

Sailors have enjoyed coming to Fairhope Yacht Club for its good harbor, well run races, camaraderie, great parties, and the best Bushwhackers in the whole Gulf Yachting Association.

64

Over the years there were hundreds of boats and sailors who came to compete in various regattas at Fairhope Yacht Club. This filled the parking lot, harbor, and clubhouse and created bonds with the clubs on Mobile Bay and the entire Gulf Coast.

Top left: The Dogwood Regatta was another Fairhope Yacht Club regatta. Held in the spring, it was a longstanding club tradition to have the local Dogwood Trail maids participate in the ceremonies on shore for this event.

Top right: This happy group of sailors pictured here were being recognized for having raised the most money for charity in the Caring Cup Regatta sponsored by Fairhope Yacht Club for a number of years.

Bottom left: A young sailor hones his racing skills.

Bottom right: Middle Bay light always has been a favorite landmark on Mobile Bay for sailors.

66

Far left: The largest of the regattas hosted by Fairhope Yacht Club and the other clubs on Mobile Bay in rotation has been the Dauphin Island Race which was started in 1958.

Top right: Crossing the ship channel sometimes presented racing sailors with close encounters.

Bottom right: This long distance race tested skippers' skills and endurance.

The Dauphin Island Race continues to be hosted by the yacht clubs on Mobile Bay and attracts hundreds of boats and sailors.

This large regatta has afforded some enterprising boaters an opportunity to profit.

Winning skippers in the regattas were awarded trophies of varying sizes and configurations. The awards ceremonies and bringing home the silver and bragging rights was part of the total regatta experience.

The Alabama yacht club with the most points in this race, based upon the club boats finishing first through third, has been awarded the Governor's Cup Trophy. This photo shows the winning skippers from Fairhope Yacht Club being presented this trophy.

69

Being number one was most important.

The winning sailors in another regatta from the past with their trophy. This photo shows the range of ages involved the sport of yachting.

71

Top: This Fairhope Yacht Club winning skipper included his young "Skipperette" in the awards ceremony.

Bottom: Women often skippered in these events and were well known for their sailing ability.

Even though women were not Equity members for many years, they competed in races on an equal basis in most of the regattas, both as skipper and as crew.

Women won many of the trophies both in local Fairhope Yacht Club races and in interclub competitions.

The Rhodes 19 fleet was one of the largest of the one design member owned boats. Over a dozen Past Commodores of Fairhope Yacht Club have owned a Rhodes 19 at one time or another and some still do. This is a bird's-eye view of the early fleet in the harbor with the club in the background.

Fairhope Yacht Club has hosted many national regattas. In addition to the Rhodes 19 Nationals, there were the Thistle Class Championships, the Lightning Nationals, and the Leiter Cup, to name a few.

In 1965, 1966, and 1967 Fairhope Yacht Club sailors won the Rhodes 19 Nationals competition three years in a row. This was not the only time a first was taken in a national class regatta, but the only triple-year win. Both men and women skippers from Fairhope Yacht Club were held in high regard nationally.

Over the years, the Rhodes 19 has been and continues to be a boat for all ages for many members and their families.

Fairhope Yacht Club also had a large Hobie Cat fleet. Here, Hobie Cats are shown on the beach prior to a national regatta held at Fairhope Yacht Club.

The starting line for a Sunfish National regatta hosted by Fairhope Yacht Club. This regatta was very successful and Fairhope was asked to host the event again.

The Laser National at Fairhope Yacht Club also received high marks from all involved.

Top left: The Leiter Cup Regatta brought young women from all over the country to Fairhope to compete in one of the most prestigious regattas. Volunteers provided food and housing, in addition to the race course work on the water and entertainment on the shore.

Left: The volunteers in this photo served on one of the many Race Committee boats overseeing the running of each race. Other volunteer jobs covered in the pre-race registration aspects of a regatta, the securing of trophies and t-shirts, and planned entertainment activities and food.

Fairhope Yacht Club volunteers have been one of the most important factors in the success of all Club activities including the running of large national regattas.

Members have volunteered their boats for many Club activities including regattas.

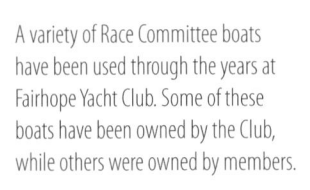

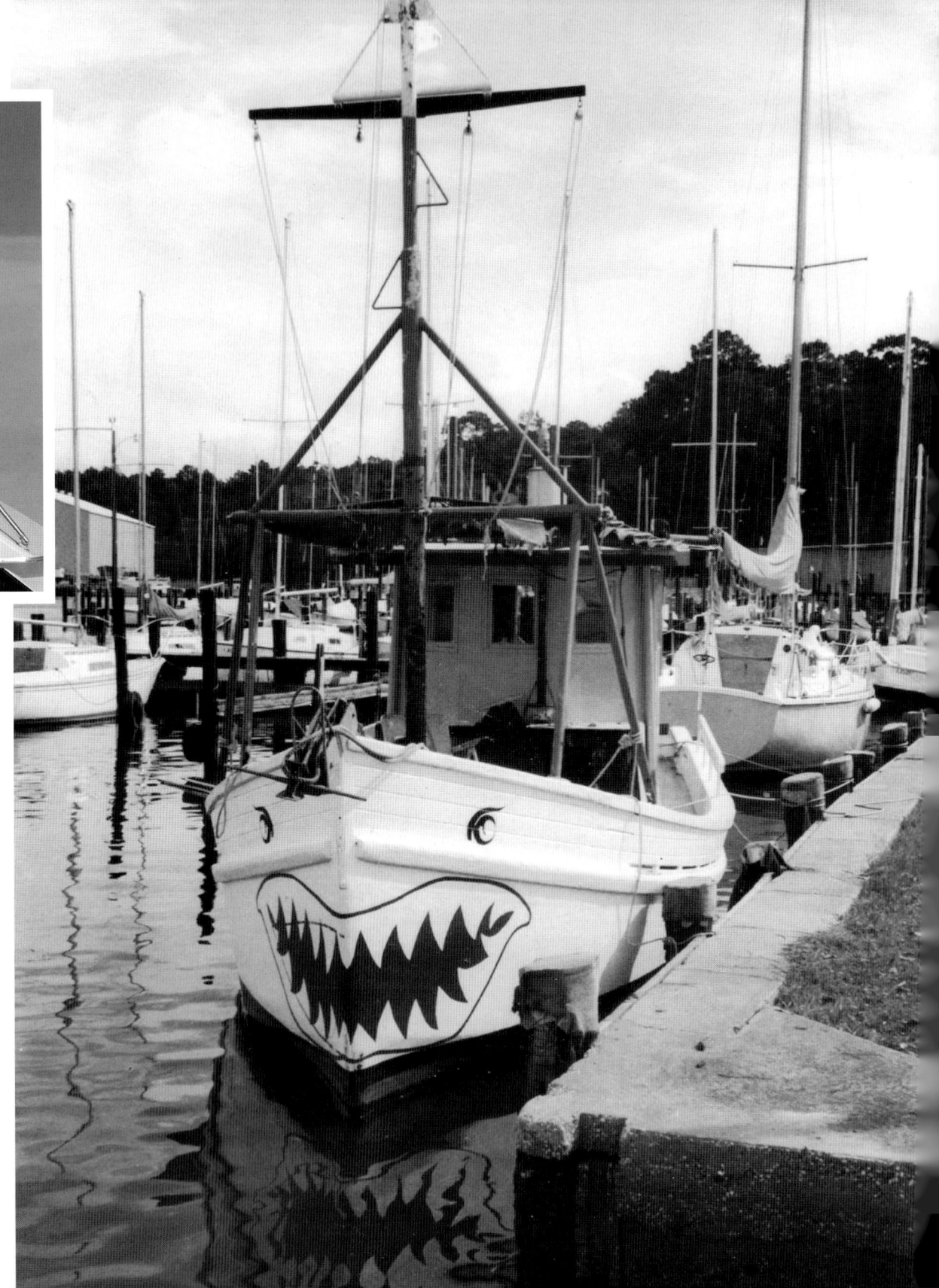

A variety of Race Committee boats have been used through the years at Fairhope Yacht Club. Some of these boats have been owned by the Club, while others were owned by members.

The A. J. Koppersmith Guardian (so named in honor of a Past Commodore) in this photo is the Club-owned boat that has been used for many years as a Race Committee boat. As with the old building, the boat has had several upgrades and engine replacements.

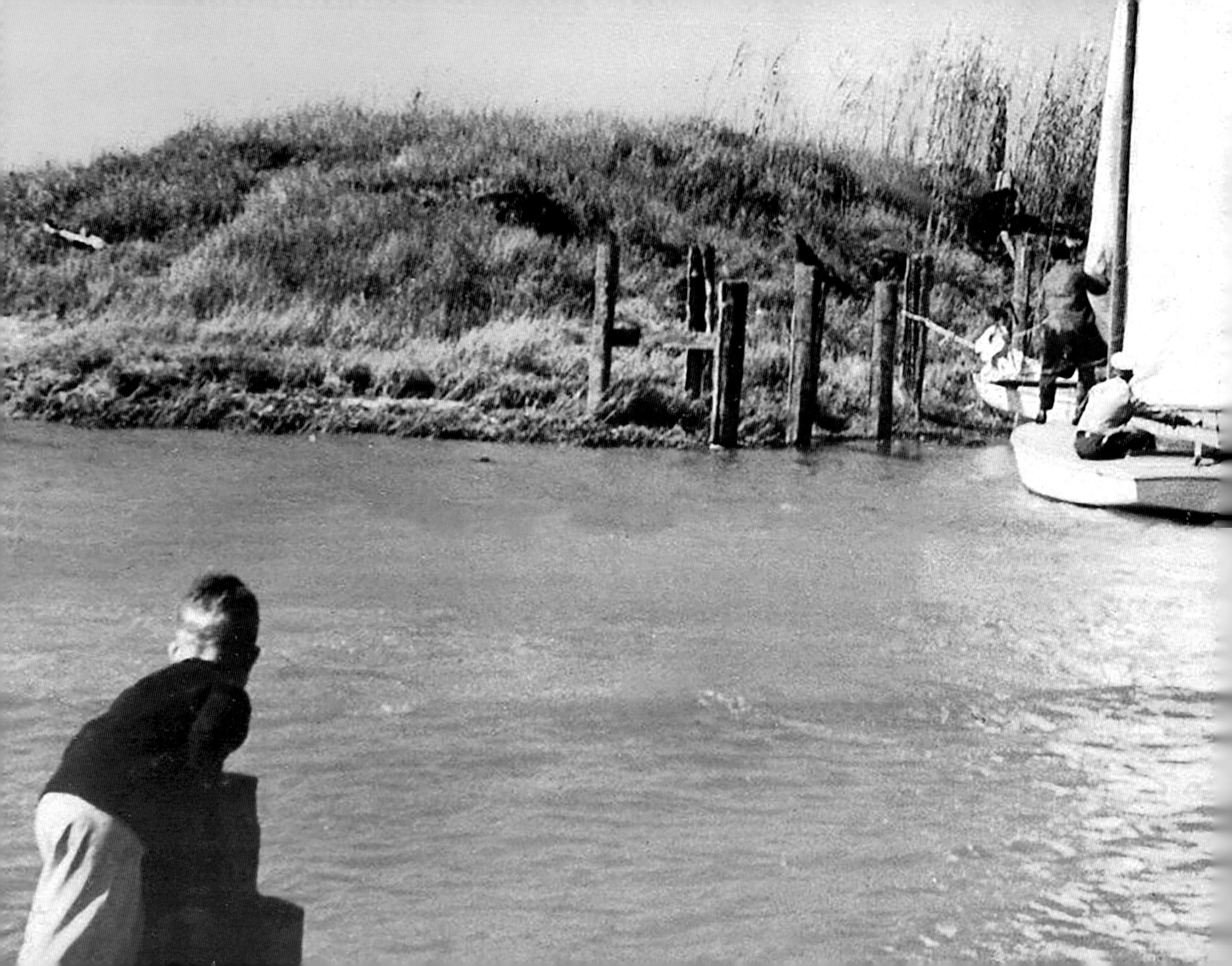

CHAPTER 8

FAIRHOPE YACHT CLUB YOUNG SAILORS

For many, boating is a lifelong love starting from an early age. And so it was for the children who came to Fairhope Yacht Club. The Fairhope Yacht Club sponsored a Junior Program for the children of members and nonmembers. The mission was to promote youth sailing and boating and safety on the water.

Children of Fairhope Yacht Club founders were involved in the boating activities along with their parents. These children were in the pram sailing group. They were not Fairhope Yacht Club Junior members yet because at this time a young sailor had to be twelve years old to join. "Pram Island" as it was called can be seen in the background.

Fairhope Yacht Club children were provided a variety of enjoyable activities including summer sailing lessons and pram races.

Top left: These youngsters were looking forward to casting off.

Top right: Pram sailing offered many young sailors their first opportunity to experience the freedom and exhilaration of flying across the water.

These children were having fun on Mobile Bay "simply messing about in boats" out from the mouth of Fly Creek.

Adult members often taught young sailors. This is a photo of a Sailfish which was an early smaller predecessor of the Sunfish.

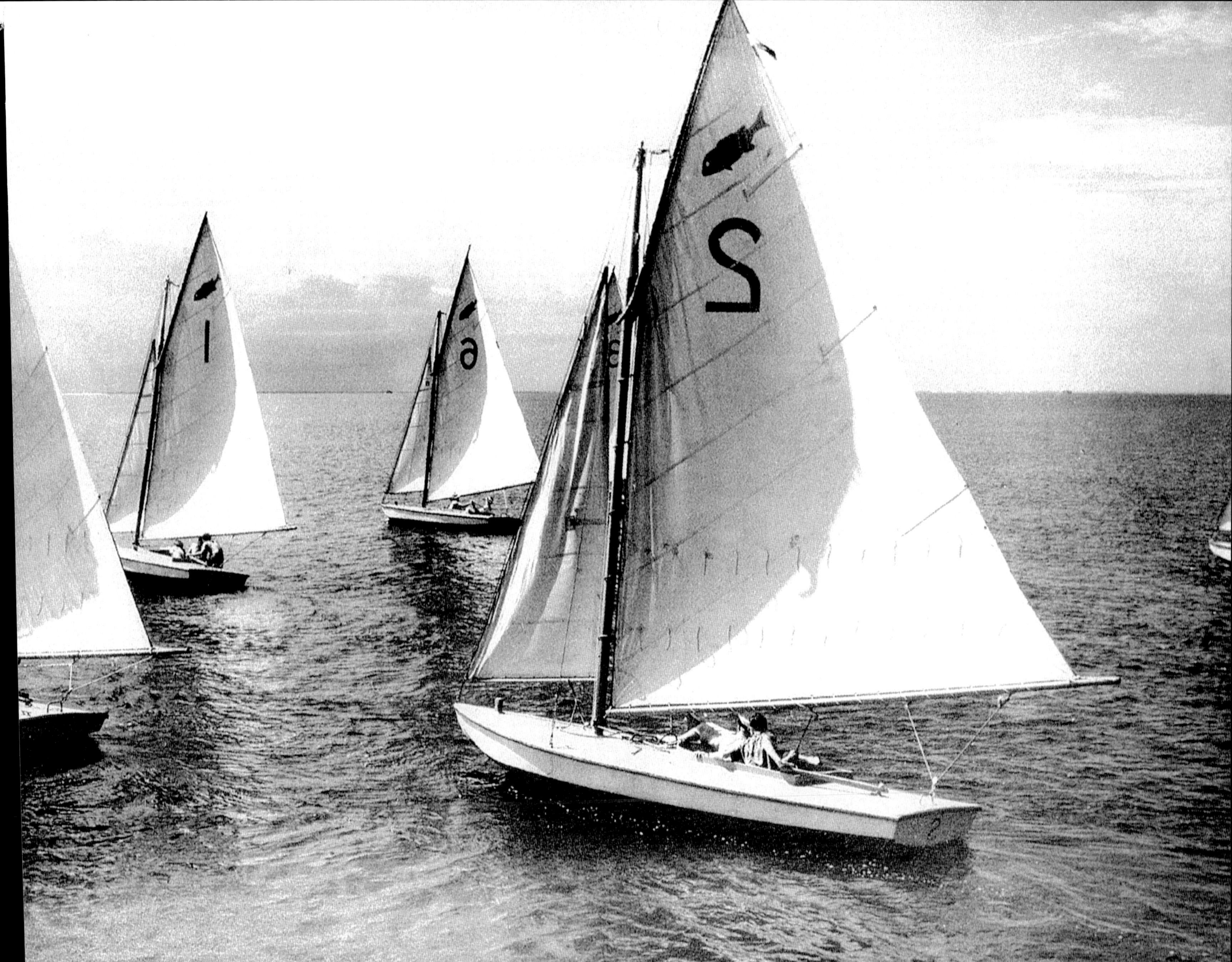

In 1947, the Fairhope Junior Yacht Club was formed. These young people were some of the first members.

Early Juniors also became involved in Gulf Yachting Association activities. In the early 1950s these Junior "Skipperettes," as they were called, had placed first in a race in the GYA's all women's Knost Regatta. This photo was proudly displayed in the original building.

Not to be outdone the male Junior members also brought home the silver in many regattas. The Fairhope Yacht Club Juniors won the famed GYA Junior Lipton Regatta three years in a row in the early 1950s.

By the 1960s, the Fairhope Junior Yacht Club grew to over one hundred members, many of whom still belong to Fairhope Yacht Club.

Fairhope Yacht Club Juniors in the 1960s posed with the trophy they had been awarded in an interclub regatta.

Often it was expected that Junior members would crew for the adults in races. This included being able to help rig the boat being sailed. In this photo a Junior member received a trophy for crewing on a winning boat.

The news article accompanying this photo refers to Fairhope's "crack" Junior sailors. Another winning boat had two Junior crewmen.

Fairhope Yacht Club Juniors were expected to help with boat care and maintenance. Here a group cleaned the bottom of one of the Club-owned boats before a regatta.

Many Juniors, as they became adults, joined Fairhope Yacht Club. There are several families with third- and fourth-generation members.

Fairhope Yacht Club Junior members worked to raise money for their programs. This group washed cars to purchase the new Sunfish here.

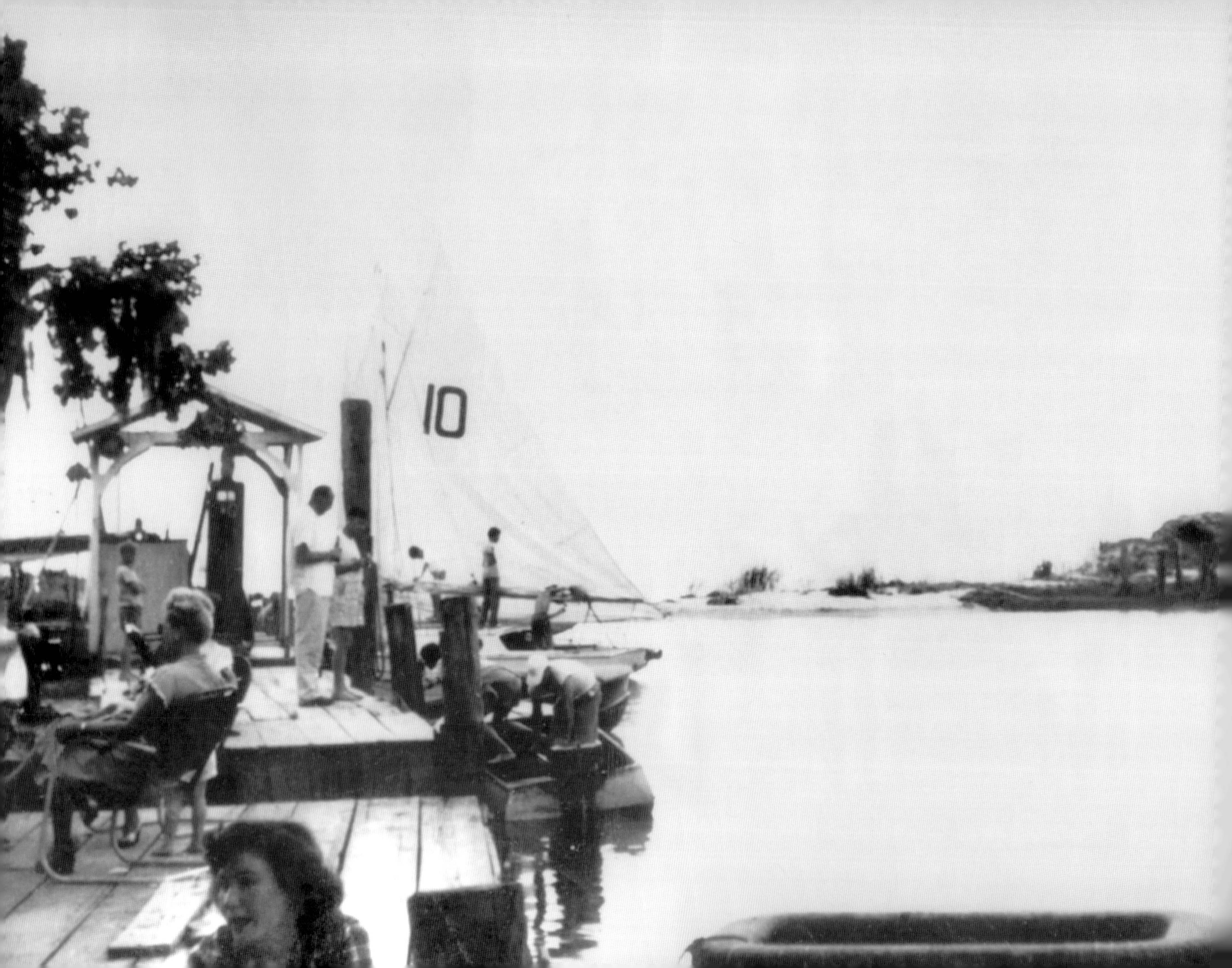
10

CHAPTER 9

FAMILIES AND SOCIAL ACTIVITIES

Talking and singing, laughing and loving, living. . . . Fairhope Yacht Club was born of families who had gathered on the banks of Fly Creek. It was an outgrowth of their shared interests and their desire to pass on the good times on the water and the bonds of fellowship to their children and to future families who would come to enjoy what they had established. Many of their social activities focused around the waters of Fly Creek and Mobile Bay.

The children who came to Fairhope Yacht Club enjoyed playing on the beach near the mouth of Fly Creek, swimming and fishing in its cold waters.

Under a parent's watchful eye, this toddler played on the beach bordering Mobile Bay. Glimpses of the first clubhouse and early harbor can be seen in the background.

Far left: A wide variety of fun activities were planned for the members' children. This photo was from the Fairhope Yacht Club Youth Fishing Tournament which awarded prizes for the smallest, largest, and mostest fish caught. Only fish caught on FYC premises were eligible. The prams used by the youngest sailors can be seen in this photo.

Top right: Young children always were included in all manner of boating activities.

Bottom right: The best swimming hole in Fairhope was located outside the north side door of the original yacht club building. These boys were cavorting on one of the lifeboat rings that had been employed as makeshift diving platforms.

Many early member events included cookouts and picnics. In this photo, the men were cooking on the Club grounds. From the attire of one of the cooks it appears that this may have been a fairly "formal" evening.

Top right: In this photo, the "Skipperettes," as they were called, were all in natty nautical dress at this feast on the grounds. They stepped up to volunteer where needed in support of the growth of the Club. Some early scheduled events included dinners, dances, and above all cocktails on Sunday afternoons.

Bottom right: In the early days and beyond, wives of members regularly provided covered dishes for potluck suppers and outdoor dining for their families, for it would be many years before Fairhope Yacht Club had a working kitchen.

FAIRHOPE YACHT CLUB

Anchorage & Club House Bayou Volanta
FAIRHOPE (On Mobile Bay) ALABAMA

January 1, 1955

Dear Mr. and Mrs. Simmons,

This notice is to remind you that dues are payable on January 1, 1955 and will be delinquent after February 1, 1955, as per the Constitution and By-Laws of your club.

The constitution specifies a $5.00 penalty for reinstatement if dues become delinquent. It is probable that if there are extenuating circumstances, or situations beyond the control of an individual they will certainly be considered by your Board of Governors.

At a special meeting of the membership, the constitution and by-laws were amended making it compulsory for a member's wife to have a membership in the club. Therefore, line two, below, covers the dues of the wife of a member.

Please help the Treasurer and pay your dues promptly.

1. Mr. dues $10.00
2. Mrs. dues $10.00
3. Pledge 1955 ....$_____
4. Federal Tax on 1955 Pledge ....$_____
5. Total Here $20.00

Just for your record, the balance remaining on pledge and tax after payment of above is $ __00__ .

Very truly yours,

FAIRHOPE YACHT CLUB

Lester I. Boone, Treasurer

For a time in the 1950s wives were required to join the Fairhope Yacht Club Auxiliary. Their dues were equal to the dues paid by the gentlemen members. With the admission of women as equity members in the 1980s membership in the Auxiliary declined.

Here are two photos of Club Auxiliary members modeling the latest styles featured at the annual fashion show.

The concrete block structure of the old clubhouse with jalousie windows can be clearly seen here.

Other shows involving fashion also delighted the membership.

According to a report at the time there were eight lovely participants competing for the title of Miss FYC before an overflow crowd. It was such a popular event that a prediction was made that the contest would become a regular part of the tradition at Fairhope Yacht Club.

FAIRHOPE YACHT CLUB

Ship Wreck Dance

...PRIZES FOR BEST COSTUME

○ DAN COOK and BAND ○

SATURDAY NITE THE 3RD

Be sure to make reservations for "Buffet Supper" as usual, Thursday Night

YACHTSMANS FROLIC
&
BOAT SHOW
REAL ORCHESTRA MUSIC.
SAT. MAY 26.
9-TILL-1
FREE
OUTBOARD MOTOR AS DOOR PRIZE
- INFORMAL -

WHERE ?- YOUR YACHT CLUB-FAIRHOPE

Top left: Various other sorts of entertainment were offered for the adult members.

Top right: Always popular, Saturday night dances were regularly scheduled.

Bottom right: The adult members enjoyed the numerous diversions available. There were parties, potluck dinners, card playing, cocktails at sunset, and always good friends and fellowship. When they visited other Gulf Yachting Association clubs, they brought burgees back to hang in the clubhouse.

Bottom right: A yachting theme played a role in many social events planned for the members.

Dancing the night away.... The jukebox played as a couple danced under the vaulted ceiling and old ships wheel chandelier.

Inset: It was said that the largest flotilla to enter Mobile Bay since Farragut's arrival in 1864 was that of the Eastward Ho cruisers. Each year in the late 1940s and the early 1950s numerous power boats from the Gulf Yachting Association clubs to the west of Mobile Bay cruised in company from New Orleans toward Pensacola and sometimes beyond.

Stops at Fairhope Yacht Club on the journey east and or on the journey back to the west occasioned parties and social activities. Here some of the cruisers had just pulled into Fly Creek. Finding dockage on Club-owned property on both sides for the great number of large vessels often filled the creek.

FAIRHOPE YACHT CLUB
EASTWARD HO
1955

LAND HO!
tie your bow and check your stern - welcome ashore at Fairhope Yacht Club

SHORE TAXI SERVICE
the "hot canary" taxi service is free for the asking - open air service hold your hat.

ICE WITH
à la bar - cheers et à votre bon santé.

SUNDAY DANCING
roy and his boys on the foredeck for your enjoyment, from 8:30 - until.

CUSTOMS AND ASSISTANCE
look for the wearers of the white ribbons
- service deluxe -

ICE AND MILK
ice and hangover medicine delivered to your yacht - call a junior yachtsman or a skipperette.

SUNDAY DINNER AT 7:00
barbecue chicken with all the trimmings - don't reduce, you need the weight for ballast -

MONDAY TAXI SERVICE
monday from 9:00 until 11:30 the drivers last trip is to the dentist, unless there is one aboard.

Above: Looking up the creek to the east. This is the view the Eastward Ho travelers would have seen.

Top left: This photo was taken during one of these stops. The harbor and parking lot were filled to capacity by this visit.

This photo shows Fly Creek taken from the high bluffs looking down the creek to the west.

105

One year all the America's Junior Misses came to visit and to take a cruise on Mobile Bay. Note the dredge in background.

Left: In later years there was a house band—The FYC Notes. The band stayed together for a number of years providing in-house entertainment and listening pleasure.

Bottom left: Each year Santa visited Fairhope Yacht Club, usually arriving by boat with his bag of toys for good girls and boys.

Bottom right: Potluck dinners remained popular even after there was a formal kitchen and restaurant open five days a week. At one point a decline in bar revenue led to the Club being closed on Monday and Tuesday evenings. The formation of the "Monday Night Pot Luckers" brought enough business to the bar to justify keeping the Club open on those nights. This tradition continues today.

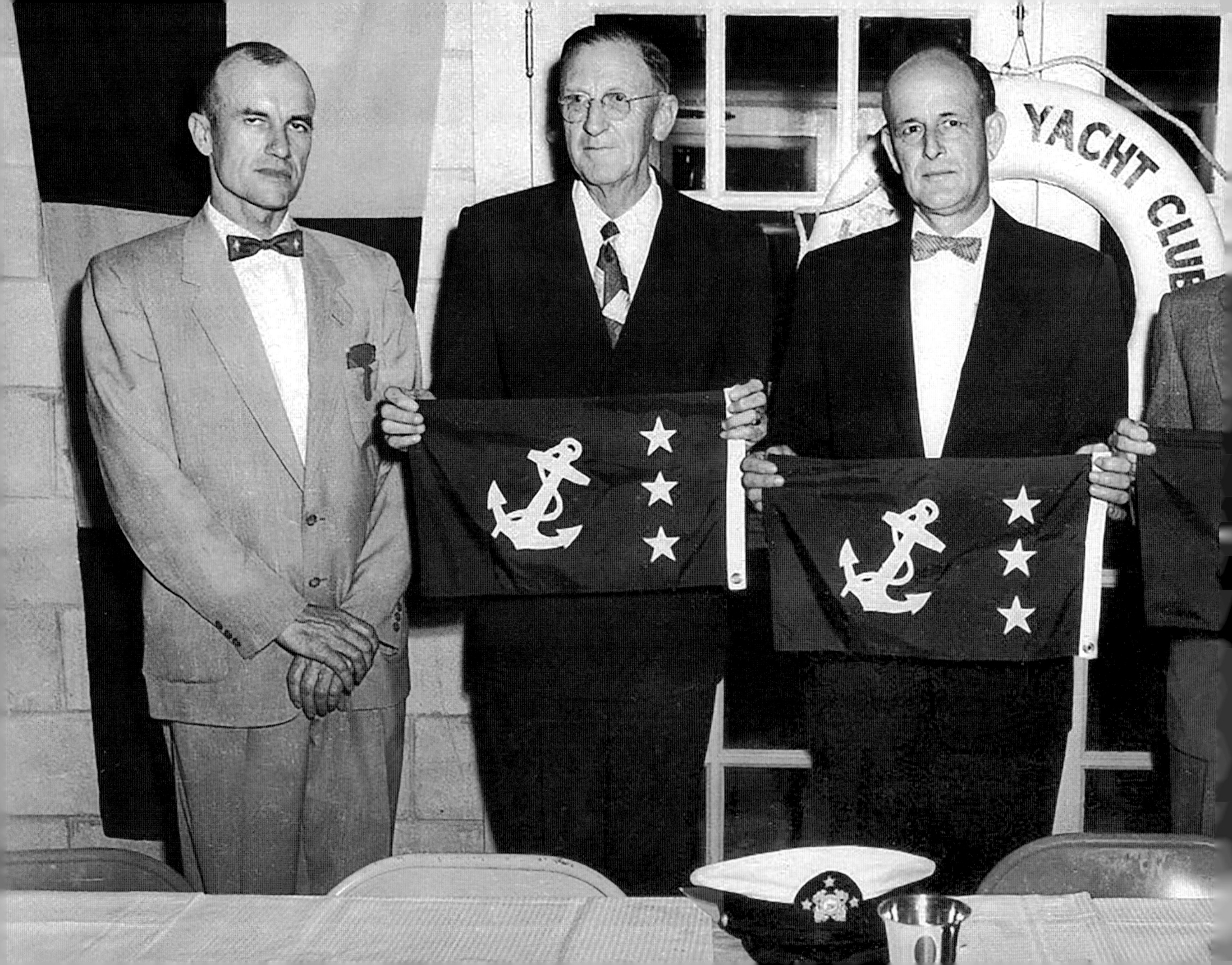
YACHT CLUB

CHAPTER 10
COMMODORES

Leadership of any organization is an integral component and so it has been with Fairhope Yacht Club. Starting in the years before the Club was formed, continuing through the early years and onward to the present, the leadership and guidance of the Commodore has been critical to the survival, continued growth, and success of Fairhope Yacht Club. There have been various traditions in place to acknowledge the service and contributions of these individuals.

The changing of the guard has been marked by different formal and informal ceremonies. Past Commodores here are being recognized by the current Commodore at a Commodore's Ball. This tradition has continued.

109

Top left: Over the years the tradition of presenting other recognition awards at the Commodore's Ball evolved. At this Commodore's Ball the Ed Coley Award for outstanding service to Fairhope Yacht Club was presented to the person selected for that year.

Bottom left: Another tradition that continues today is the annual Commodores' Cup Race for the Past Commodores. Different one design boats have been used in this annual race where Past Commodores compete against one another. Races that were held in Sunfish and prams provided much entertainment to all.

Top right:: Past Commodores seen here were enjoying a toast after the race. The Past Commodores had stories to tell about the events of the day, reliving the race. The stories were enhanced with each toast of champagne.

Above: More recently, the Rhodes 19 Class boats have been the vessel of choice. For many years when racing in the Rhodes 19s, Past Commodores drew for a boat in which to race and were required to supply crew members.

Picking a winning crew was very important.

The Commodore's Cup here shows a happy face on one side for the winning Past Commodore and a sad face on the other for the losing Past Commodores. The winner of the Past Commodores' Race is presented the cup filled with the adult beverage of choice at the end of the race and has his or her name added to those of the other winners on the base of the trophy.

Far left: The tradition of presenting the Commodore's Cup to the winner of the Past Commodores' Race also continues.

Top right: Always, Past Commodores have shared a special fellowship with each other. This group had gathered around the fireplace to thaw out after a particularly cold wet race.

Bottom right: Past Commodores posed in front of the old ships wheel which had been repurposed as a memorial for deceased Past Commodores.

Fairhope Yacht Club Commodores always have maintained a good working relationship with the mayor and Fairhope city leadership.

This aerial photo of the Fairhope Yacht Club property on the north side of Volanta Avenue shows the building, grounds, and harbor as it was into the last quarter of the twentieth century.

FAIRHOPE YACHT CLUB PAST COMMODORES

Otto Wadewitz	1941–1945	John C. Miller	1980–1981
James E. Gaston	1946–1947	Phillip M. Chapman	1982–1983
Jack Bonnell, Sr.	1948–1949	Robert I. Mace	1984–1985
Marvin Berglin	1950–1951	A. Wes Stapleton	1986
Jack W. Bonnell, Sr.	1952–1953	Daniel l. Hamilton	1987–1988
Hoyt S. Greenbury	1954–1955	Gary A. Moore	1989
Isadore Reynolds	1956–1957	Carl Carnley	1990
Robert Young	1958	Robert Hamlin	1991
John C. Glover	1959	Robert Van Iderstine	1992
Isadore Reynolds	1960	Paul E. Ring	1993
Ed Warley, Jr.	1961–1962	Vincent Lo Presti	1994
A. J. Koppersmith	1963–1964	Thomas Y. Yeager	1995–1996
Al E. Conroe, Sr.	1965	J. Steven McClure	1997
T. Copper Van Antwerp	1966–1967	Steven J. Odom	1998–1999
Jack R. Hays	1968–1969	E. Tony Chavers	2000–2001
Joe Graham	1970	Stuart Adams	2002–2003
Robert Stine	1971	Barbara H. Brown	2004–2005
Burleigh Whiteside	1972	Thomas Y. Yeager	2006–2007
George Fuller	1973	Erik G. Schmitz	2008–2009
Wellington H. Johnston	1974–1975	Carl A. Wainwright	2010
Thomas S. Talbert, Jr.	1976	Catherine M. Cromartie	2011–2012
Charles L. Dees	1977	Dan Herzog	2013–2014
A. Wes Stapleton	1978	Gary W. Garner	2015–2016
Wes Stauley	1979	Anne Randlette Fitz-Wainsright	2017

FAIRHOPE YACHT CLUB COMMODORES OF THE GYA

Jack Bonnell	1956	Robert I. Mace	1996
Cooper Van Antwerp	1969	Catherine M. Cromartie	2016
Charles L. Dees	1988		

114

This photo was one of the last taken of the original building with all its additions and improvements that had been filled with members and memories for over sixty-three years.

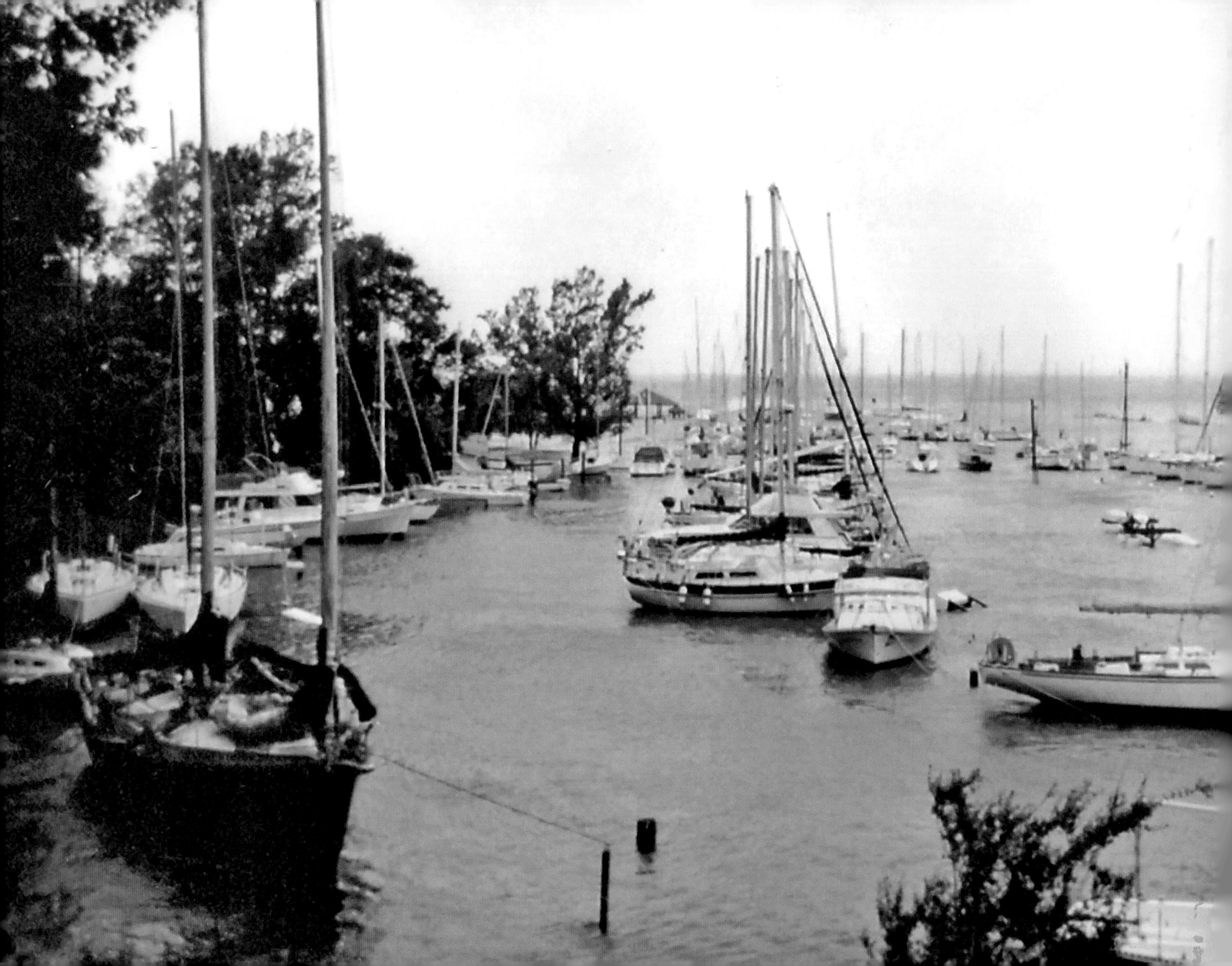

CHAPTER 11

Hurricane Katrina and Beyond

Wind driven rain pounded all night but by sunrise all was calm and clear for a while. Then water began creeping in from Mobile Bay spilling onto the Fairhope Yacht Club parking lot and drawing closer to the old building. Small animals began taking refuge on higher ground and members who had driven down to the Club to check on their boats had to move their cars, first from the large parking lot in front of the clubhouse and then again from the smaller side parking lot.

The waters rose over the island and continued to rise as the wind shifted around. As the day progressed the wind and waves pushed many boats along with the docks across Fly Creek to the Sea Cliff side. Some boats were lifted up and dropped onto adjacent pilings, other boats broke free and drifted out into Mobile Bay. The boats and docks and finger piers near and on the island were spared the worst of the destructive wave action.

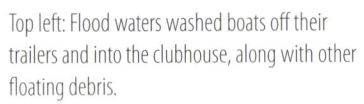

Top left: Flood waters washed boats off their trailers and into the clubhouse, along with other floating debris.

Top right: Wind and waves drove a huge waterborne log through the front of the Fairhope Yacht Club building causing the collapse of part of roof and other structural damage.

The walls on the Fly Creek side of the clubhouse were completely destroyed.

Top left: Rising as high as eight feet inside the decades old edifice, furniture, equipment, mementos, and other treasures were flung about with abandon and left in a sodden heap.

Top right: Every part of the property was covered with sand, boats, trailers, piers, decks, docks, debris, and detritus.

As the flood of water receded, Fairhope Yacht Club members were sick at heart to see what had been left behind.

This aerial photo of Fly Creek taken just after Hurricane Katrina showed the extensive damage done to the outer harbor and building and grounds. Boats and docks were scattered over on the opposite creek bank also and sand covered everything.

The pier on the south side of Volanta had just been repaired following the damage done by Hurricane Ivan the previous year. This is the what was left by Hurricane Katrina.

Hurricane Katrina not only damaged the property at Fairhope Yacht Club, but affected the local wildlife including the beaver living in a pond just south of Volanta. This pelican was unable to fish after the storm and was provided fresh caught fish for as long as needed to regain its health again.

Under one of the remaining oak trees, a place to rest and relax from hours of clearing and cleaning was carved out in the sand, allowing members to refresh, recover, and commiserate.

From this simple gathering place, another meeting spot under the roof of the former BBQ pit was fashioned by Club members from salvaged lumber. Nearby was a single working water spigot and a newly installed power pole with a small electric box which provided limited electricity.

Barely a month after Hurricane Katrina, the Wadewitz Regatta Skippers' meeting, party and trophy presentations were held in this reclaimed area. Visiting Gulf Yachting Association sailors from along the Gulf Coast expressed their gratitude to Fairhope Yacht Club for hosting this GYA regatta. They were able to come to race and to have a good time and leave their own troubles behind for a time.

The small boat storage loft on the property on the south side had been seriously damaged during the storm, but was structurally sound. With member-donated labor, salvaged parts from the old clubhouse, and reclaimed washed-up lumber the little building was quickly refashioned into a new clubhouse for Fairhope Yacht Club.

Members donated labor, materials, electrical work, appliances needed to chill the beer. . . . A Past Commodore installed windows in the boat barn, a member donated all the electrical work, another member contributed appliances that continue to be used today, and so on. . . .

Top left: Families continued bringing their children to be introduced to the joys of sailing.

Top right: The Junior Yacht Club remained active with programs for young sailors.

Another Sunfish National Regatta was hosted.

This period in the history of Fairhope Yacht Club is looked upon by many as the best of times, when everyone was brought more closely together by what was not available. During this time of adversity Fairhope Yacht Club traditions continued.

The sunsets were better than ever.

Top left: Meeting the challenges presented, the Fairhope Yacht Club continued to provide food, entertainment, regattas, both local and national, and a viable meeting place for its members.

Top right: For three years, Fairhope Yacht Club's entertainment activities and programs in the boat barn and on the grounds were very successful in sustaining the membership and in bringing together many diverse groups.

Bottom left: The little building and surrounding picnic area often was filled to capacity and beyond with more members socializing than ever before.

Again, there was no kitchen or even a formal bar at first or any of the amenities members had come to expect. Potluck dinners with the Club providing the meat and communal dinners from the BBQ grill on the grounds became the norm.

Top left: Fairhope Yacht Club's dedicated office manager and bar manager worked alongside the members throughout the entire process of recovery and rebuilding. They played a major role in providing continuing services to the membership.

Top right: Somehow Santa still could find his way to Fairhope Yacht Club, although he had to be rowed in.

Families enjoyed the casual atmosphere of the boat barn clubhouse just as the early families had come to love their old clay tile building.

The Ed Coley Service Award and other traditional awards were presented in the tent at the Commodore's Ball.

Top left: And he had to meet the children in a tent in the parking lot to hear their wishes and to distribute the gifts in his pack.

Bottom left: The Commodore's Ball also had to be held in a large tent for the next few years. The first was on a cold December afternoon, with two working water spigots and two power poles providing ample food and beverage service to over four hundred celebrants.

Top left: Fairhope Yacht Club Past Commodores came together in the Boat Barn for the traditional Commodores' Cup Race.

Top right: Again, the Rhodes 19's were the boat of choice for their race.

Right: And again, there was dredging to be done.

130

50 Years of Sailing
Dauphin Island Race ~ 2008

HOSTED BY FAIRHOPE YACHT CLUB
ALONG WITH MOBILE YACHT CLUB, BUCCANEER YACHT CLUB AND LAKE FOREST YACHT CLUB, INC

Boats sailed past the Middle Bay Lighthouse landmark.

The 50th Anniversary Dauphin Island Race was hosted by Fairhope Yacht Club during this interim period. All related parties and activities took place in the parking lot, in tents and in temporary structures. It was a huge success in spite of the problems encountered.

Fairhope Yacht Club members and Past Commodores had stepped up to provide help in many ways after the storm.

The coveted GYA Offshore Challenge Cup Regatta was again won by Fairhope Yacht Club and a new trophy was brought home.

A Past Commodore agreed to serve again, as several had before, to help lead the club through the planning and construction phase ahead. Past Commodores also served on the Building Committee and the Finance Committee working to rebuild the clubhouse.

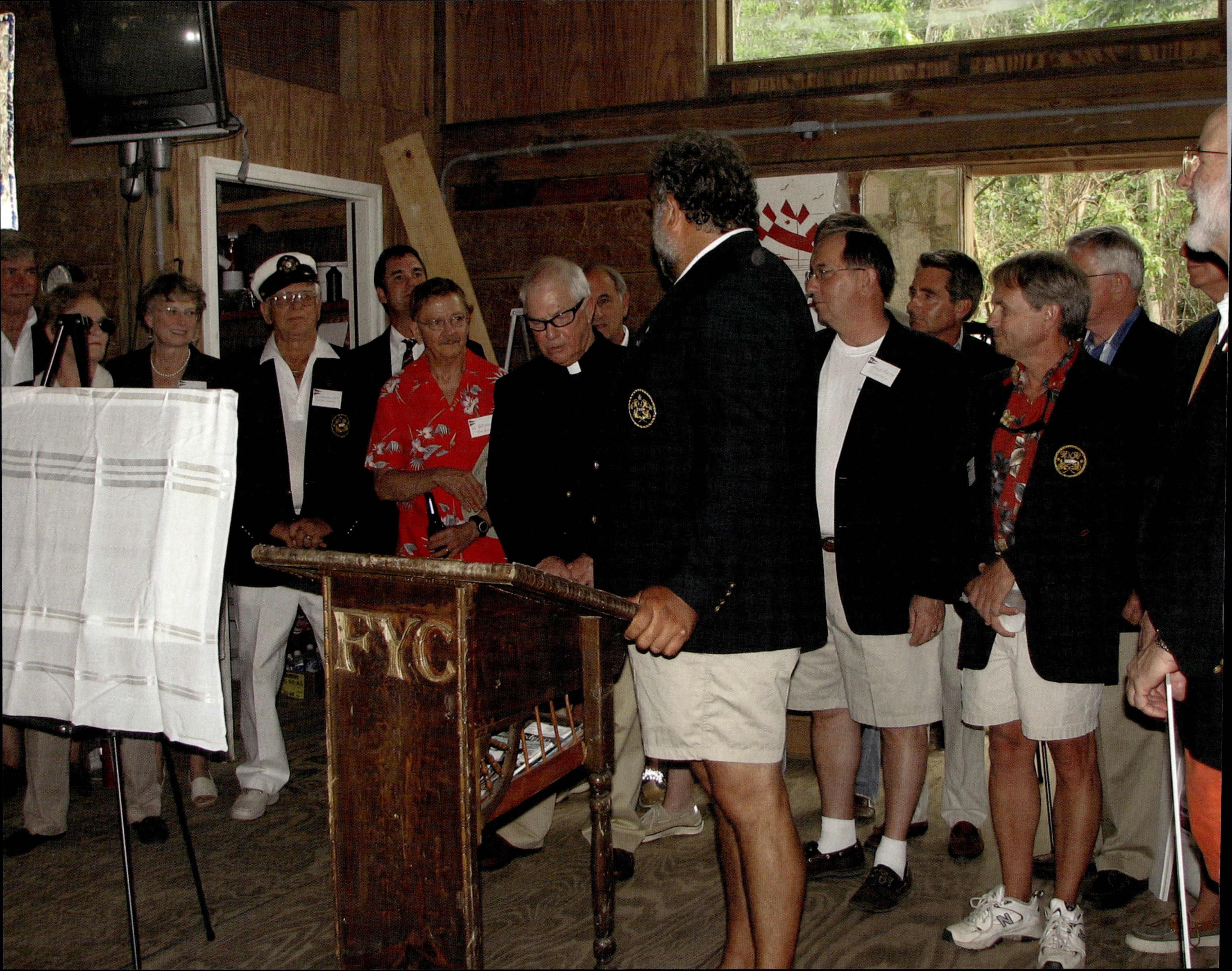
FYC

This new building would reflect the rich architectural heritage of the Gulf Coast.

During the process of planning and building for the future, a swimming pool to be located on the island was voted in as the newest addition to the Fairhope Yacht Club physical plant.

The Building Committee worked with engineers and architects to design and build a new clubhouse to meet current code requirements and the needs of the membership. The Finance Committee worked to plan a way to pay for it.

135

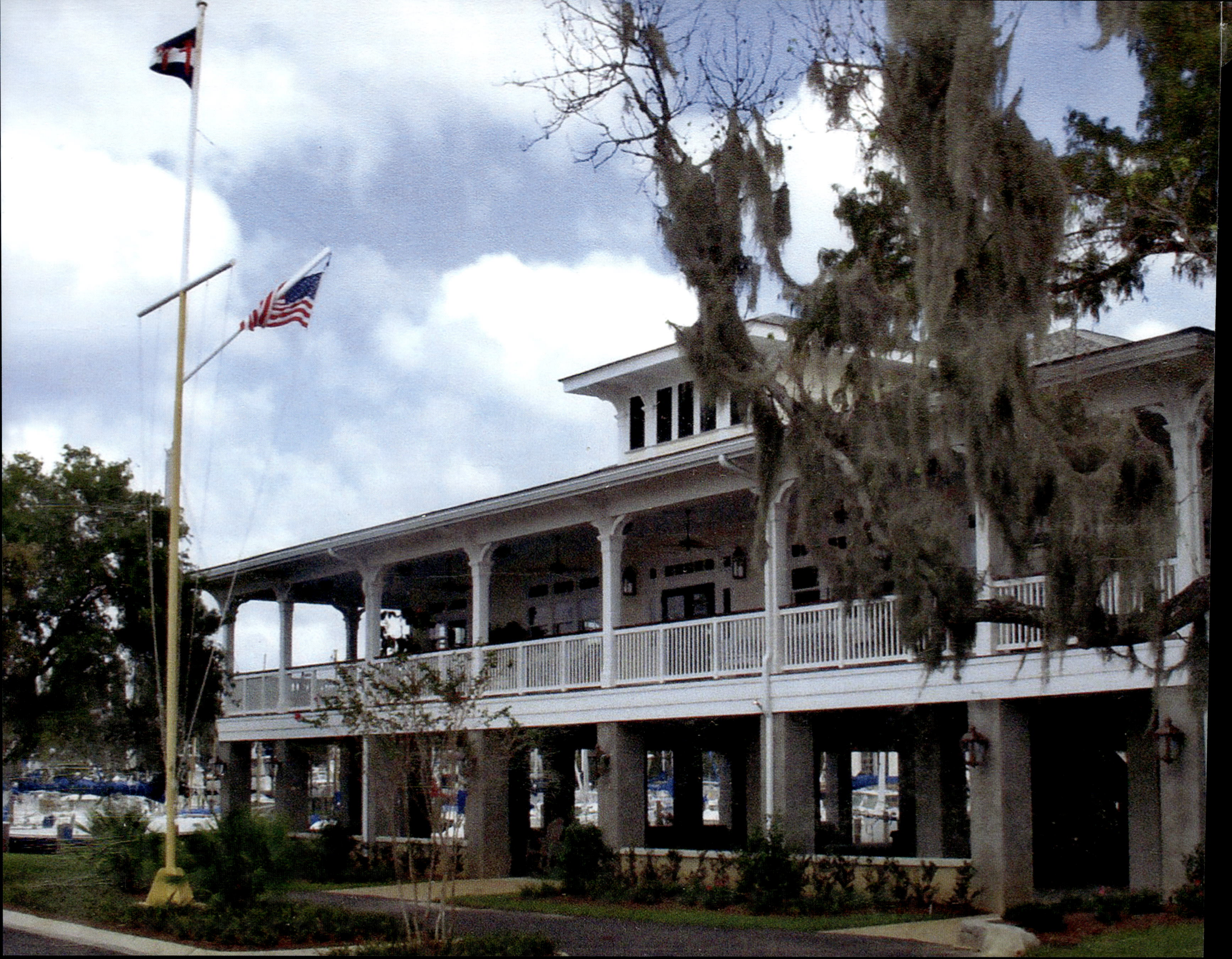

CHAPTER 12

SAILING INTO THE FUTURE

Finally on August 29, 2008, the third anniversary of Hurricane Katrina's destruction, the Gulf Yachting Association Commodore and the Fairhope Yacht Club Commodore officialy commissioned the new Fairhope Yacht Club building and declared it open.

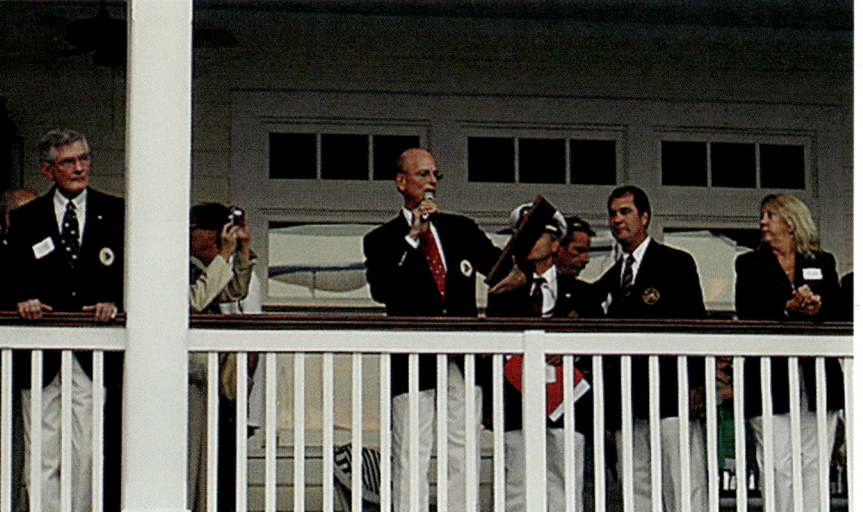

Gulf Yachting Association member club Commodores, Fairhope Yacht Club Past Commodores, and officers and members joined in the ceremony and the celebration.

Old traditions continued in the new facility as Century Heritage members were officially inducted and had their names added to the board listing those who have achieved that status.

137

Past Commodores continued to sail the Commodores' Cup Race. These Past Commodores are posed in front of the ships wheel that had served in the original building as a light fixture and then as a Memorial Wheel for Deceased Past Commodores. The wheel was salvaged after Hurricane Katrina, repaired and refinished, and now continues to provide a place honoring deceased Past Commodores.

In memory of Founding Commodore Otto Wadewitz, a Past Commodore built a model of his motor yacht Rex and donated it to the Club along with a bronze bust he had scuplted of Commodore Wadewitz.

The Ed Coley Service Award continued to be presented at the Commodore's Ball.

A new regatta was established in honor of a Past Commodore. Held in the summer, the Ring Around the Bay Regatta is a long-distance race in Mobile Bay.

Fairhope Yacht Club Junior Program activities continued to develop sailing skills.

Fairhope Yacht Club Juniors won the Gulf Yachting Association Junior Lipton Cup for the first time since the early 1950s.

Fairhope Yacht Club provided for the establishment of the only high school sailing team in the state of Alabama.

These smiling young sailors received medallions for their participation in a Club-sponsored regatta.

Three one design boats chosen by the Gulf Yachting Association for member clubs to sail in sanctioned inter club competitions can be seen in this photo. They represent the past, present, and future of GYA racing. The first one design boat selected by the GYA was the Fish Class, the second one was the Flying Scot Class and the third one now being phased in is the Viper Class.

The Gulf Yachting Association Opening Ceremonies and Regatta were held at Fairhope Yacht Club again. Another Past Commodore had been elected Gulf Yachting Association Commodore.

Even after the new building was opened the Boat Barn continued to be used by various groups of members from Seniors to Juniors and for private parties.

The Doc Rogers band was the new Fairhope Yacht Club band. They have provided entertainment for many of the club regattas and parties.

Storms and flood waters will continue to visit. However, now the new Fairhope Yacht Club building is much safer from this potential threat.

Next page: And the story continues. By creating this beautiful landmark on Mobile Bay, Fairhope Yacht Club members set sail toward new adventures. By continuing to encourage the sport of yachting, to foster fellowship, and to nurture sportsmanship, they ensure the future of the Fairhope Yacht Club for years to come.

About the Authors

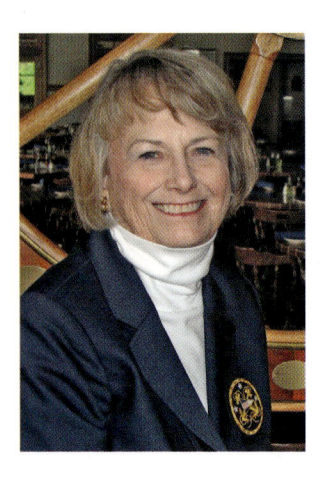

Barbara Hayes Brown, B.A., M.A., Ed.S., worked in school systems in Mobile and Baldwin Counties for thirty years and was a Consultant with the Alabama State Department of Education for over ten years. She has been an active member of Fairhope Yacht Club for nearly thirty years and during that time has served on various elected and appointed committees, including the Board of Governors, and was elected the first female Vice-Commodore and Commodore. She has been one of the Club historians for over twenty years.

Her sailing experience includes crewing on a variety of boats in many regattas and cruising on a twenty-six-foot Nonsuch sailboat across the Gulf of Mexico to various ports on the coast of Florida, to Isla Mujeres, Mexico, as well as traveling the entire Tenn-Tom Waterway.

Co-creator of the film, *A History of Fairhope Yacht Club*, she resides in Fairhope, Alabama.

Sarah Johnston Cox, B.S., M.S., by profession a teacher, has been connected to Fairhope Yacht Club her entire life. As one of the first female members admitted as an equity member, she has served on the Board of Governors, as well as on numerous other elected and appointed committees at Fairhope Yacht Club. She has been one of the Club historians for over twenty years.

An avid sailor, she sailed and skippered on the first place team in two national regattas and was a sailing instructor for the University of South Alabama.

Co-creator of the film, *A History of Fairhope Yacht Club*, she resides in her family home on Mobile Bay.

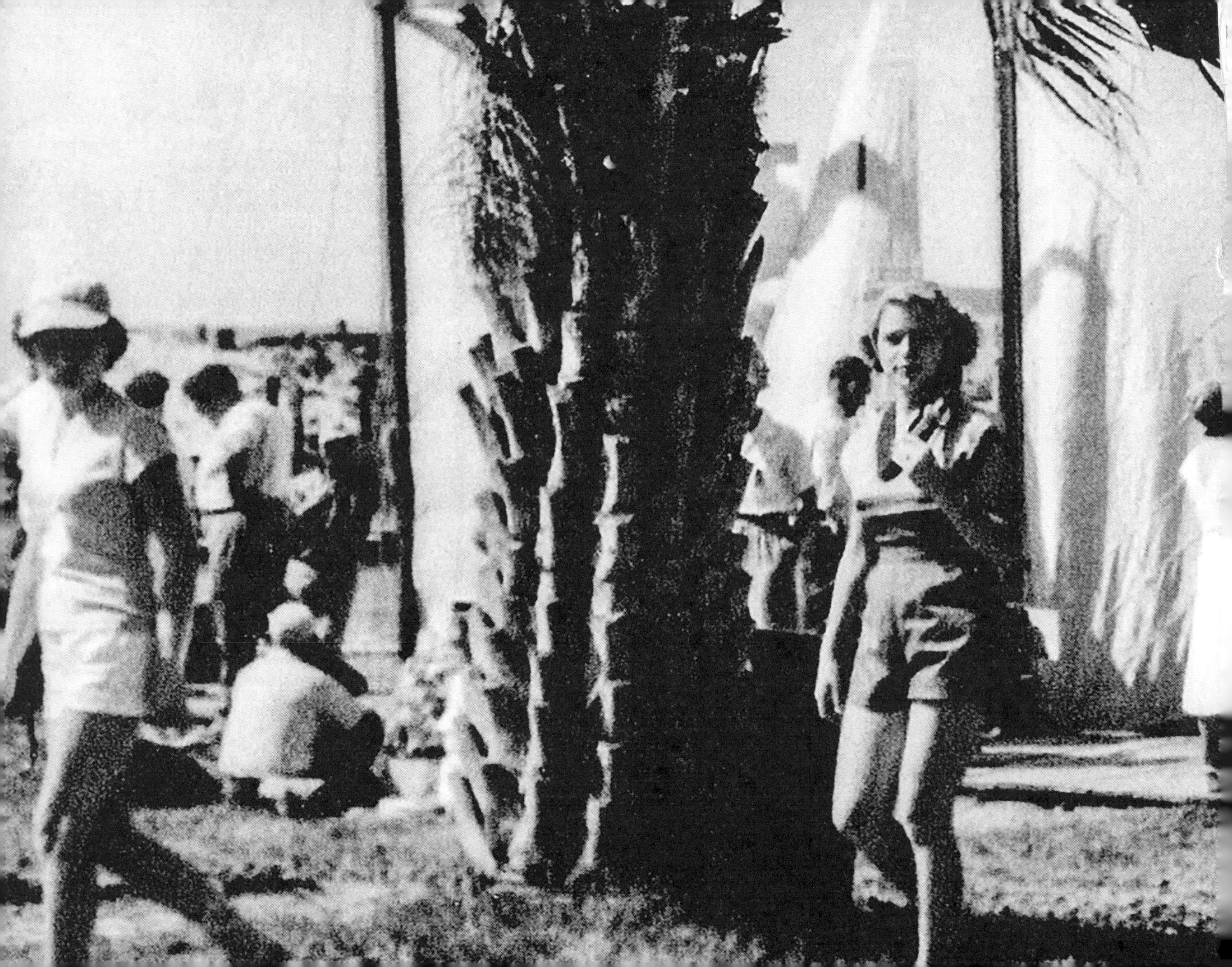